INTEGRITY SELLING
FOR THE 21ST CENTURY

Other books by Ron Willingham

The Best Seller!

Hey, I'm the Customer

Integrity Selling

The People Principle

When Good Isn't Good Enough

INTEGRITY SELLING

SELLING

FOR THE 21ST CENTURY

How to Sell the Way People Want to Buy

Ron Willingham

CURRENCY

DOUBLEDAY

New York   London   Toronto   Sydney   Auckland

A CURRENCY BOOK
Published by Doubleday
A division of Random House, Inc.

CURRENCY is a trademark of Random House, Inc., and DOUBLEDAY is a
registered trademark of Random House, Inc.

Library of Congress Cataloging-in-Publication Data

Willingham, Ron, 1932–
    Integrity selling for the 21st century : how to sell the way people want
to buy / Ron Willingham.—1st ed.
        p. cm.
    1. Selling. 2. Integrity. I. Title: Integrity selling for the twenty-first
century. II. Title.

HF5438.25.W534 2003
658.85—dc21   2003043844

ISBN 0-385-50956-1

Book design by Erin L. Matherne and Tina Thompson

PRINTED IN THE UNITED STATES OF AMERICA

FIRST EDITION: July 2003

SPECIAL SALES
Currency Books are available at special discounts for bulk purchases for
sales promotions or premiums. Special editions, including personalized
covers, excerpts of existing books, and corporate imprints, can be
created in large quantities for special needs. For more information,
write to Special Markets, Currency Books, 280 Park Avenue, 11th floor,
New York, NY 10017, or email specialmarkets@randomhouse.com

20 19 18 17 16 15

*My sincere thanks to all our Integrity Systems Business Associates,
certified facilitators, and clients around the world. You've provided
the real-life learning experiences for this book to be at the
cutting edge of professional, customer-focused selling success.*

A Special Thanks

I must thank four people without whose help this book couldn't have happened.

First to Anita Matas for her many hours of word processing, proofing, and correcting the manuscript. Her superior intelligence, over mine, helped out time and again.

To Robyn Doty for help in proofing, correcting, and word suggestions.

To Roger Scholl, my Doubleday Senior Editor who made this relationship easy and enjoyable.

To Jane Dystel, my superagent, for her professional work with the publisher.

Contents

Definitions

Selling   A process of identifying and filling people's wants or needs that creates mutual value for customers, salespeople, and their organizations.

Integrity   The quality of being complete, whole, sound. The quality of living out sound moral principles, uprightness, honesty, sincerity.

Integrity Selling   A win-win customer-focused process, driven by honesty and sincerity; creating mutual value for sellers and buyers.

Customers   Anyone whose wants or needs you fill. You may call them clients, patients, guests, members, associates, or internal staff whom you serve.

Integrity Selling Values and Ethics

1. Selling is a mutual exchange of value.
2. Selling isn't something you do *to* people; it's something you do *for* and *with* them.
3. Developing trust and rapport precedes any selling activity.
4. Understanding people's wants or needs must always precede attempts to sell.
5. Selling techniques give way to values-driven principles.
6. Truth, respect, and honesty provide the basis for long-term selling success.
7. Ethics and values contribute more to sales success than do techniques or strategies.
8. Selling pressure is never exerted by the salesperson. It's exerted only by customers when they perceive they want or need the item being recommended.
9. Negotiation is never manipulation. It's always a strategy to work out problems—when customers *want* to work out the problems.
10. Closing is a victory for both the salesperson and the customer.

Preface

Henry S. Golding once wrote:

What our deepest self craves is not mere enjoyment, but some supreme purpose that will enlist all our powers and will give unity and direction to our life. We can never know the profoundest joy without a conviction that our life is significant—not a meaningless episode.

Selling with integrity provides purpose for salespeople. It helps us enjoy a more professional and meaningful life. We experience high self-esteem, genuine joy, and exhilarating enthusiasm for life when we look past our own needs and focus on filling those of other people.

As we sell with integrity.

Introduction

What is the key to success in selling?

Why do some people succeed at it and others fail? Why do at least 80 percent of all salespeople reach plateaus and stay there? And what does this cost them and their organizations in lost income or profits?

Why do some salespeople struggle while others in the same organization, selling the same products or services, in the same market, earn into the hundreds of thousands of dollars?

Why are billions of dollars spent on sales training each year by organizations of all sizes, only to find that most of what they spent was wasted? Why is it that much of what's taught to salespeople not only doesn't get results but actually prevents them from selling well?

Why do most sales training programs, seminars, or books on selling present it as a series of strategies, gimmicks, or attempts to control behaviors—all designed to get a potential customer to say "yes"? They teach ridiculous strategies like "nail-downs," "tie-downs," "open probes," "closed probes," tricky closes, ad nauseam. Yet anyone who's ever sold anything soon discovers that continued success in selling is 85 percent emotional and only 15 percent strategy.

Many Questions, Many Answers

Selling isn't driven by knowledge or skills alone—although they are a necessary foundation. The truth is that knowing how to sell doesn't improve people's ability to sell. Rather, successful selling is largely driven by deep emotions—our beliefs, our values, our awareness of our own capabilities, and our feelings of self-worth. Most salespeople know this intuitively; unfortunately, most don't know how to build on this intuitive knowledge.

If you've tried manipulative, self-focused selling techniques and felt that they demean both you and your customer, or if you've ever wondered if selling could be more than just talking people into buying whatever you're selling, you'll find this book a breath of fresh air. You'll not only learn how to sell in a highly professional way, you'll also feel better about who you are. Most important, your ability to achieve higher levels of success will increase.

Integrity Selling is a process that both you and your customers will feel good about doing. It's doing the right thing for people. When you sell with integrity, you don't approach people with the intent of selling them something; rather, your goal is always to gain rapport and understand their objectives so you can help them get what they need.

Integrity Selling is doing something *for* people rather than *to* them. Its focus is to create value for customers. It's all about them, not you. Paradoxically, you sell more with this selfless attitude. To get to the heart of the matter—Integrity Selling begins with *who you are*. I believe that when your values, motives, and desire to help your customers are right, your actions and behaviors will be right. Customers want to do business with people they can trust. That's why strong ethics and values contribute more to selling success than strategies and techniques.

How do I know this for a fact? I once observed several hundred salespeople who were taught to use deceptive practices like bait and switch, and encouraged to play negotiation games with customers. They were so stressed by this behavior that they suffered from a high incidence of alcohol and substance abuse, divorce, job-jumping, and low productivity. In the same industry, I have observed countless people who had been taught to sell with high integrity. Ironically, their customer satisfaction, profit margins, and salesperson retention were significantly higher.

This book debunks many old selling myths. It contains the appropriate mix of customer-focused sales skills with the psychology of personal achievement. I'll reveal to you the core traits of all highly successful salespeople, and give you Action Guides to practice that will help you develop these very traits.

If you'll walk with me, I'll guide you to a more highly successful future—one filled with higher goals, increased sales, and greater confidence.

I know that you're skeptical, and you should be.

It's up to me to earn your confidence and respect.

I believe I can do that.

How I've Earned the Right to Help You

I've been selling since I was ten years old. I love it. Except for two months in my adult life when I received a salary, I've been paid a commission or I've owned my own business where my compensation depends on how much I sell and earn.

Since I founded my current organization, Integrity Systems, Inc., in the mid-1960s, nearly two million people have taken our courses in over sixty-five nations. Over 25,000 facilitators have been certified to conduct our courses. This comprises over 2,000 organizations of all sizes—from the Chevrolet Division of General Motors, where 26,000 people learned Integrity Selling in the first year, to organizations with only fifteen to twenty people.

I continue to work with clients in order to stay well aware of the tough issues that salespeople face—and so I can continue to improve and refine selling techniques that work in the real world.

As you assimilate and apply the Integrity Selling principles, you too will succeed in the real world of selling.

Integrity Selling Gets Results

I often get glowing feedback from people who have completed the Integrity Selling program. They have applied the concepts in their selling with outstanding results. I could give you hundreds of examples, but here are just a few:

The North Atlantic Region of American Red Cross reported a 35 percent increase in blood sales after implementing Integrity Selling. Employee turnover dropped 50 percent.

Mike Niedert, top manager of the Principal Financial Group, Des Moines Agency, reported a 33 percent increase in agent production, and an astounding 50 percent four-year retention of agents. The industry retention average is around 14 percent.

Larry Cowles of MassMutual reported a 25 percent increase in sales at his agency after initiating Integrity Selling.

Before offering Integrity Selling to their dealer population, Chevrolet piloted it with twelve select dealers of all sizes. This resulted in an increase in closing ratios of 25 percent and a gross margin increase per sale of 31 percent.

Dave Benfield of Infinite Energy in Gainesville, Florida, wrote, "When I joined the company and trained my salespeople in Integrity Selling, we had fourteen thousand customers. Fifteen months later, we have more than fifty thousand! We've had virtually no turnover and our margins have been handsome."

After training their people in thirty-five nations with Integrity Selling, Trade New Zealand reported a whopping increase of $500 million in trade with other nations.

A large division of Johnson & Johnson reported a 26 percent sales growth rate in Japan and 28 percent in South Africa. Their Holland representatives are enjoying 15 percent more time with doctors.

AIM Funds, a mutual fund company in Houston, Texas, wrote that for every dollar they invested in Integrity Selling, they enjoyed $195.00 in new sales.

In one region of a large national insurance company, the people who practiced Integrity Selling sold over three times the actual health policies sold by their associates, with much higher per policy premiums.

All over the world, salespeople, by using Integrity Selling, are enjoying increased sales and customer loyalty. Real people like Rene Vugts of Holland, Borek Navratil of the Czech Republic, Roberto Azevedo of Brazil, Teruaki Ueda of Japan, Zvika Gildoni of Israel, Tor Gjersvold of Norway, Charbel Mouawad of Dubai, and thousands of others. They all have one thing in common—Integrity Selling has become part of their lives.

What You'll Learn

Of course you didn't pick up this book, nor will you continue to read it, because of what I or the thousands of our course graduates have done. So let's talk about what you will learn about sales and selling as you put my ideas into action and make them a part of your daily routine:

1. The four core traits that all highly successful salespeople possess, and how to develop them.
2. Why your selling success is largely the result of unconscious beliefs rather than conscious knowledge.
3. How to identify and relate to different styles of people.
4. How to gain quick rapport with people and get them to drop their defenses.
5. How to focus your sales strategy on your individual customers' needs rather than on your own need to make a sale.
6. How to get people to trust and want to do business with you.

7. How to *listen* people into buying, rather than *talk* them into buying.

8. How to increase your confidence, energy, and "achievement drive."

9. How to develop *motivational intelligence* to empower yourself and propel you to higher sales levels.

10. How to present yourself to customers so you stand out above the crowd of competitors.

11. How to develop a powerful "prosperity consciousness" that allows you to focus on the rewards you hope to gain as a result of your hard work.

12. How to deal with negative situations that could otherwise zap your confidence.

You will also learn to use:

1. A six-step customer-focused selling system that teaches you to judge how much time to talk and listen, as well as the steps that must be completed before a sale can be made.

2. A Sales Congruence model that shows you which of your values, beliefs, and personal character traits must be in harmony for you to sell at higher levels and enjoy permanent customer trust and loyalty.

3. A common, everyday Behavior Styles language so you can easily communicate with all types of people.

4. A Dimensions of Human Behavior model to understand where your knowledge, feelings, habits, and unconscious beliefs come from. You'll learn what few people know about the *source* of what I call "prosperity consciousness."

5. A Progression of Human Needs model so you can identify and focus on the different needs and levels of need people have.

You'll learn many other things as well—all useful guidelines that will help increase your ability to sell at significantly higher levels than before.

The Six-Step System of Selling

In addition to its customer needs–focused philosophy, Integrity Selling teaches you a six-step selling system. Whether you're a rookie salesperson or an experienced veteran, you'll find this system easy to understand, yet constantly challenging. Here are the six steps:

Approach . . . to gain rapport

Interview . . . to identify needs

Demonstrate . . . to explain how features and benefits will
  satisfy those needs

Validate . . . to prove your claims

Negotiate . . . to work out problems

Close . . . to ask for a decision

Six steps. Approach, Interview, Demonstrate, Validate, Negotiate, and Close.

I call it the AID,Inc. system. You can remember AID,Inc. if you remember that it's a sales *aid* that helps you be more successful when you *incorporate* it into your selling. AID,Inc. stands for Approach, Interview, and Demonstrate. To make Validate, Negotiate, and Close fit "Inc.," we'll have to bend the way we spell "validate." Spell it val-I-date, and pronounce it val-eye-date. That gives us the "I" to go with the "N" and the "C."

The graph on page xxiv represents the AID,Inc. system:

In Chapter 2, you'll learn three rules for using this system, along with how much time to talk and listen at each step. Each chapter will explain every step in detail and offer you Action Guides for practicing them.

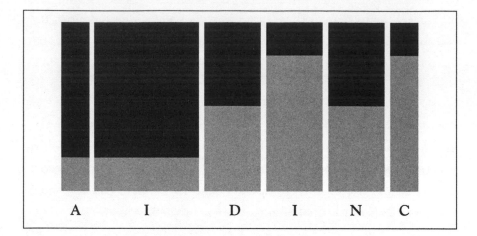

Cultural Changes, Value Shifts
Demand Greater Integrity

In my original *Integrity Selling* book (Doubleday, 1987), I presented a basic customer-focused selling philosophy, along with the AID,Inc. system that helped salespeople carry out this philosophy. The book shared what I had learned from real-world experience since I introduced the selling system in 1980. We redefined selling from "a process of convincing people to buy from us," to "a process of identifying and filling needs people have."

My organization was a pioneer in this new concept of selling, and we experienced a lot of "tough sledding" with managers who were looking for "closing skills" for their salespeople.

Looking back, we were riding on a huge tidal wave of change that would forever redefine the way people did business. The real estate and banking crashes of the mid-1980s. The flexing of customers' muscles, kicked off by Tom Peters and Robert H. Waterman, Jr.'s, classic *In Search of Excellence*. The fall of the Berlin Wall. Savings-and-loan scandals. Technology exploding into everyday life and its accompanying new techno-language. The banking industry redefining itself. High tech creating overnight Nasdaq paper billionaires, before imploding. Enron, WorldCom, Global Crossing, Arthur Andersen, etc.

We've just certified a group of Johnson & Johnson sales managers in Warsaw, Poland, to conduct Integrity Selling for their sales reps. All these managers grew up behind the Iron Curtain in the Soviet bloc countries. Until the late 1980s, they never heard of "free enterprise" or knew anything about selling. They were extremely excited, open, and receptive to our program.

Changes. Incredible, phenomenal social and economic changes— many of them pleading for answers to the question "Where did all the integrity go?"

Since my first *Integrity Selling* book was published, my organization, Integrity Systems, has trained salespeople and managers in over sixty-five nations, in all sizes of organizations. We've learned many things about successful selling that we didn't know fifteen years ago.

We have Integrity Selling graduates going to surgical rooms and advising surgeons about difficult new procedures. Some course graduates sell basic products; others sell highly complicated technology. In a sense they all do the same thing. They identify and fill customers' needs, focusing on creating value for them.

It's always been this way for highly successful salespeople. It will always be this way, regardless of changes.

Previous to 1980, my training and development background was focused on the psychology of personal growth. I absorbed everything I could from great thinkers like Dr. Carl Jung, Dr. Carl Rogers, Dr. William James, and other great human development thinkers. For seven years, I worked with Dr. Maxwell Maltz, author of the best-seller *Psycho-Cybernetics*. I learned much about his concepts of self-image psychology and how to apply them in my courses.

I've learned that successful selling isn't an issue of knowing how to sell; rather, it's one of self-beliefs, values, positive attitudes, and profoundly deep emotional factors.

You'll learn all these success factors in this book.

"The More I Learn, the More I Learn There Is to Learn!"

School is never out for the professional who constantly strives to improve and to enjoy higher and higher levels of success and quality of life. What you'll learn in this book, when practiced in your everyday selling, will work for you—whether you're a rookie just entering your career, or a seasoned pro.

I must also stress that this book is meant to be *practiced*, not just *read*. Your increased sales will result from *changed behaviors*, not increased *knowledge*. To achieve maximum benefits from each chapter, please follow these suggestions:

1. Scan the entire book first to get an idea of its content.
2. Come back and spend one week reading and rereading one of the chapters. Chew on the thoughts, digest them, think how you can apply them.
3. Underline key points, make notes on the pages, and write down Action Guides or other ideas on index cards. Carry them as reminders.
4. Then spend one week on each chapter doing this same active process.

This will help you convert the concepts I discuss to automatic behaviors. Only as you do this will you enjoy steady increases in your sales and self-beliefs.

And finally . . . please take a moment, close your eyes, and picture how substantially increasing your sales, customer loyalty, and confidence would improve your life.

Picture some goals that you'd really like to reach but that deep inside you haven't believed possible. Keep these images in mind. Don't evaluate their actual possibilities. Suspend any critical evaluation. Just keep visualizing them, along with the rewards you'll enjoy when you reach them. Remind yourself of these rewards several times each day. Let me assure you that if you're willing to work to get them, I'm going to help you enjoy them.

If you apply the Integrity Selling concepts to your selling, you'll enjoy higher sales, stronger customer relationships, growing self-confidence, and expanding "prosperity consciousness." You can hold me to this.

So . . . get prepared to move ahead of the herd.

[1]

The Four Traits of
Highly Successful Salespeople

You've been introduced to the basic six-step Integrity Selling process, AID,Inc. But before we begin to learn the steps, we need to take a closer look at the psychology of selling, and what drives successful salespeople.

To begin, I'd like you to take a short quiz.

Please write on a sheet of paper your best answer to the following questions:

1. What distinguishes highly successful salespeople from others?
2. What do high achievers do and think that lesser ones don't?
3. What are the deepest core traits that highly successful salespeople possess that the wanna-bes don't?

I've asked many people these questions. In many cultures. In many types of businesses. Their answers are usually logical ones like: Highly successful salespeople make more calls, they manage their time better, they have a winning personality, or they have better products or services. They're enthusiastic. They have positive attitudes. They work smarter, and so on.

While all these answers contain a certain element of truth, they don't explain why one salesperson sells ten times the amount of another person with equal knowledge, experience, and training. External behaviors like enthusiasm, time management, and a good personality are actually driven by deeper causes. After observing thousands of salespeople, in all kinds of cultures, businesses, and economic climates, I believe that there are four core traits that the high producers have that others don't. More than anything else, these central traits drive their successful beliefs and behaviors:

1. Strong Goal Clarity
2. High Achievement Drive
3. Healthy Emotional Intelligence
4. Excellent Social Skills

Let me briefly describe each of these.

Goal Clarity—this means having clear, specific, written goals of what you want to have happen in your future. They must be goals that you deeply desire, and most important, goals you firmly believe are possible for you to achieve, and that you feel you deserve to achieve.

Achievement Drive—this is a latent, potential power that everyone has. It usually stays dormant within most people because they lack goal clarity. But once you have clear goals that you passionately want to reach, deeply believe to be possible, and feel worthy of achieving, you automatically release this energy according to the intensity of your inner beliefs and desires.

Achievement drive causes persistence, a dogged determination, and a never-give-up attitude. It drives you to learn what you must do to be successful, and then motivates you to develop the necessary skills to reach higher goals.

Emotional Intelligence—this is basically two things:

1. It's the ability to understand the emotions you're feeling (and those of others) and their impact on your behaviors. It helps you identify fear of rejection and its numerous emotional cousins that, if allowed to rule your actions, can kill your success. People with high emotional intelligence are better prepared to deal with negative emotions, resistance to change, and other success killers.
2. Because it gives you such strong self-awareness, it also allows you to have the inner discipline to do things that you often don't want to do, but must do in order to be successful.

Social Skills—these have little to do with talking, or having the "gift of gab." They're more about communicating with people—asking questions, listening, understanding, having empathy and rapport.

Great communicators have the ability to identify people's different Behavior Styles and adjust to them. They can see the world through other people's eyes and think, move, and make decisions like others do. When you develop this kind of rapport with people, they'll trust and respect you more, and they'll subconsciously want to buy from you.

To the extent you possess these four traits—Goal Clarity, Achievement Drive, Emotional Intelligence, and Social Skills—you'll sell well. Strengthen them, and you'll automatically increase your current sales. Wherever you are on a success curve, you'll discover that the more you develop these core traits, the more you'll discover your potential for further development.

Self-Evaluation

The following self-evaluations will give you a general idea of how you rank in these four traits. Obviously these aren't exhaustive, validated measurements; rather, they suggest some basic behaviors related to the traits.

Please read each statement and evaluate how descriptive it is of you from 1–10.

Goal Clarity	Never		Sometimes		Always
1. I continue to write down clear, specific goals for sales and income.	1 2 3 4 5 6 7 8 9 10				
2. I revise and update my goals each month.	1 2 3 4 5 6 7 8 9 10				
3. My goals are consistent with my values.	1 2 3 4 5 6 7 8 9 10				
4. I feel worthy of achieving higher goals.	1 2 3 4 5 6 7 8 9 10				
5. I break my goals down into small daily steps.	1 2 3 4 5 6 7 8 9 10				
				Total = _____	

Achievement Drive	Never			Sometimes				Always		

1. I demonstrate a very
   high level of desire for
   higher goals.   1 2 3 4 5 6 7 8 9 10

2. I am self-motivated
   and committed to
   high achievement.   1 2 3 4 5 6 7 8 9 10

3. I fully believe that my
   goals are within my reach. 1 2 3 4 5 6 7 8 9 10

4. I constantly plan rewards
   for myself to motivate me
   to reach my sales goals.   1 2 3 4 5 6 7 8 9 10

5. My need for achievement
   overpowers my fears
   of rejection.   1 2 3 4 5 6 7 8 9 10

Total = _____

Emotional Intelligence	Never				Sometimes				Always	
1. I am driven by a strong sense that I create value for people above what they pay me.	1	2	3	4	5	6	7	8	9	10
2. I maintain a level emotional response despite ups and downs.	1	2	3	4	5	6	7	8	9	10
3. I understand my emotions and their influence upon my sales behaviors.	1	2	3	4	5	6	7	8	9	10
4. I am able to pick myself up again after repeated rejections or missed sales.	1	2	3	4	5	6	7	8	9	10
5. I have learned how to replace negative emotions with positive ones.	1	2	3	4	5	6	7	8	9	10

Total = _____

Social Skills	Never		Sometimes		Always
1. I adjust well to different types of people and situations.	1 2 3	4 5 6	7 8	9 10
2. I listen well and am sensitive to people's ideas and needs.	1 2 3	4 5 6	7 8	9 10
3. I am especially effective at calming people in stressful situations.	1 2 3	4 5 6	7 8	9 10
4. I am highly intuitive— able to pick up people's unspoken meanings.	1 2 3	4 5 6	7 8	9 10
5. I work well with a wide diversity of people.	1 2 3	4 5 6	7 8	9 10

Total = _____

What Does My Score Mean?

The scores of your self-assessment aren't that important. My purpose for offering these self-assessments is:

1. To help you understand specific behaviors that contribute to each trait.
2. To evaluate how descriptive each statement is of your actual behaviors.

Later in this chapter, you'll learn how to select statements from these assessments and develop them as habits.

The Beginning of High Achievement

Goal Clarity—your ability to define and reach higher goals—is driven by your deep, emotional need to succeed, a need that causes you to want to earn more, have more, or be more. It's usually the hope of gain or the fear of pain that drives you to strive for higher goals.

Often as we set and begin working on goals, a natural resistance to change sets in that can make us settle for the same goals we've always had. It's hard to let go of our well-established, safe, secure comfort levels. It's just easier to keep the status quo. To not run risks. To not rock the boat. To settle for what we've been settling for.

If you've ever been kept from reaching your goals by self-limiting thoughts, you're not the only one. The truth is that the moment you set higher goals, you trigger the following emotions:

1.   Initial excitement—the thrill of new possibilities can be intoxicating until you realize how much extra effort is usually required before change can take place.
2.   Conflict—you might wonder, "Can I actually achieve this new goal? What if I try and fail?"
3.   Doubt—focusing on the difficulties or roadblocks, and wondering whether you can overcome them.
4.   Resistance to change—the idea of changing your habits, beliefs, and routines becomes uncomfortable.
5.   Commitment—a renewed sense of dedication to whatever work, learning, or effort it might take to reach your new goals.
6.   Acceptance—finally believing deep down that you're capable of reaching your new goals.

People who successfully reach their goals almost always experience all six of these emotional stages. Many people, however, get stalled out in the second, third, or fourth stage, and progress no further. Then, to prevent any future pain of failure, they unconsciously quit setting goals. They opt to stay where they are and remain at that comfort level.

Stages two to four are formidable emotional barriers we must move through before we can fulfill our dreams. Goal achievement is largely an emotional or self-esteem issue. We can reach only the goals that our self-beliefs allow us to achieve. So the real challenge lies in enlarging our own internal pictures of *what* we're *capable* of achieving, and *what* we *deserve* to have.

Reaching Goals Is a Matter of Inner Congruence

Reaching goals isn't just a matter of knowing how. It's a much deeper issue. Here are some typical inner conflicts that could limit your performance:

- *Setting a goal that conflicts with your values.*
- *Setting a goal that you don't really believe to be within your possibilities.*
- *Negative environment—friends, family, or associates—that keeps you discouraged and emotionally fragmented.*
- *Not really believing that higher goals are possible, which causes low energy and achievement.*

Until these conflicts are worked through, you'll release little effort toward reaching your goals.

But once you begin to build an inner belief that your goals are possible, that you deserve to have them, that they're congruent with your values, and that you have good support systems, you automatically release a new energy, an *achievement drive* from deep within you.

Releasing Your Achievement Drive

Achievement drive is energy that's released from within you once you have goal clarity. This is what separates you from the pack. Your achievement drive continually increases as you strengthen your belief that you're capable of reaching your goals and that you deserve the benefits and rewards that they'll bring you.

Without strong achievement drive, people set goals but don't attain them. If our self-image isn't high enough to allow us to believe that we deserve to enjoy higher goals, we'll find subtle, unconscious ways to "prove" that they're impossible for us to achieve. We wind up sabotaging ourselves without even consciously knowing it.

On the other hand, as achievement drive is released, it multiplies your other skills, knowledge, and abilities. To understand the multiplying power, evaluate your knowledge, skills, experience, education, and training using a scale of one to ten, with ten being total mastery. Then add up these four numbers, and multiply by your achievement drive rating to get your "success power." Success power indicates your potential for reaching high goals.

	Knowledge	_____
+	Skills	_____
+	Experience	_____
+	Education/Training	_____
×	Achievement Drive	_____
=	Success Power	_____

This formula explains how, with achievement drive as the multiplier, people with equal knowledge, skills, experiences, and education or training can perform on entirely different levels. High achievement drive can carry anyone to higher and higher sales and achievement because it multiplies the net effect of all our other skills, resources, and abilities.

You must understand that achievement drive isn't released because you know about it; rather, it's the result of having goal clarity and believing the goals to be within your possibilities. You can increase your achievement drive by practicing the Action Guides that I lay out in this book in your selling experiences.

Your View of Selling

We know from observing thousands of salespeople that their view of selling influences their achievement drive level. Generally, salespeople who view sales as a process of *convincing* customers, or doing things *to* them, have lower achievement drive. Salespeople who view it as a process of identifying and filling customers' needs experience a stronger release of achievement drive. They exhibit more energy, a stronger work ethic, and an eagerness to do the difficult activities that must be done in order to reach goals that are important to them.

Salespeople who view selling as a win-win transaction, where value is enjoyed by both seller and customer, have higher self-confidence and are less reluctant to ask customers for decisions. Achievement drive is also released from within them when they view selling as an opportunity to create value for customers and when they believe they should be rewarded in a way that is consistent with the value they create.

We release achievement drive when we have a balanced view of selling that's expressed by these attitudes:

1. I feel a professional responsibility to create as much value for customers as possible.
2. I know that I will, and should be, rewarded to the degree that I create value for customers.
3. So I will focus on creating as much value as possible for clients, knowing that I'll be rewarded accordingly.

This is a balanced view of selling that will cause your view of your own possibilities to increase, and as it does, more and more achievement drive will be released from within you.

Later in this book, I'll share other ways you can consciously release more of this powerful energy.

The Need for Emotional Intelligence

As you begin to emotionally believe in higher goal possibilities, and you begin to release achievement drive, the need for healthy emotional intelligence kicks in. Emotional intelligence produces traits like stability, steadiness, persistence, even-tempered control, and the ability to deal with rejection.

Let's face it . . . selling isn't always easy; we often get rejected. We face many unknowns. We stick our egos out for people to accept or stomp on. Fear of rejection, and fear of what might happen that we don't want to happen, can be formidable enemies. They probably cause more failure in selling than any other single reason.

My first job after college was as an outside salesman at an office supply and equipment store. I had all the confidence in the world when people came into the store. But when I went out to call on them, I'd suddenly experience a very strong, almost paralyzing fear of rejection. I remember driving around and around different clients' office buildings, silently hoping that I wouldn't find a parking spot.

Shortly, because I was working on a straight 10 percent commission, I came to grips with the fact that avoidance wouldn't pay the bills. I had just married, had a new car, apartment, and television payments. I brought to this marriage thirty-five dollars in total assets. I hate to brag, but, well, it was all cash.

One day it dawned on me that if I allowed my fear to rule my actions, I wouldn't sell anything. So I forced myself to go into purchasing agents' offices and make calls—even though it took all the discipline I could muster at that time. I've since learned that many people experience the same emotions, but if they give in to these natural feelings, they'll fail.

Those were difficult but valuable learning experiences. I learned that emotional intelligence can be developed—if we're willing to pay the price for getting it. One way it's developed is by doing the things you fear to do.

"Do the thing you fear and the death of fear is certain," wrote William James, the father of modern-day psychology. Understanding and controlling our emotions is essential for moving ahead into higher and higher levels of goal achievement.

Throughout this book, I'll share many actions you can practice that will help you to develop this valuable trait.

Social Skills Help Us Relate to People

Social skills are demonstrated when you ask questions and listen, when you understand different behavior or communication styles, and when you adjust your natural style to fit other people's styles. It's the ability to understand the unspoken. To read body language. To pick up on voice tones, inflection, and facial expressions. It's being able to intuitively crawl inside other people, then think and see the world as they do. It's the willingness to listen to people without biases. To understand their viewpoint. To suspend your view of how things are and understand their beliefs and opinions. Excellent social skills help us jump on board other people's trains of thought and ride with them as co-passengers.

Practicing the communication Action Guides in this book will increase your social skills and improve your customer relationships, as well as build your confidence.

Why Certain Salespeople Succeed

Salespeople with high degrees of goal clarity, achievement drive, emotional intelligence, and social skills will almost always find a way to succeed regardless of product, market, territory, or other variables. As you increase these traits, your sales will almost always go up, regardless of your current sales levels.

Now, let me throw you a bit of a curve and say that these four traits can't be *intellectually learned*. Simply knowing about them doesn't mean you have them. Rather, they're *experientially developed*. You get them only by practicing certain actions in real-life situations. Only by getting into the game and getting bruised and bloody. Experiencing the agony of defeat and the thrill of victory; making a no-withdrawal commitment to higher success. Believing that rewards will come.

If these traits can't be intellectually learned, but can only be experientially developed, then two questions naturally arise:

1.   Where do these four traits reside within me?
2.   How can I develop stronger levels of them?

Stay with me, because I'm about to tell you.

The Three Dimensions of Human Behavior

In the last three decades, over one and a half million people have gone through our development courses. I've studied and observed and attempted to understand more about this complex mechanism we call *human behavior*—why some people succeed, others fail.

This practical laboratory, along with outside studies and salespeople's performance results, have helped me develop the following model. As we move through this book, this model will help you develop a deeper understanding of:

1.   Who you are.
2.   How you got that way.
3.   How to change your life and circumstances—if you choose to do so.

Let's look at three separate dimensions within us. They are the:

1.   Intellectual
2.   Emotional
3.   Creative/Unconscious

To further understand each dimension, please look at the following model:

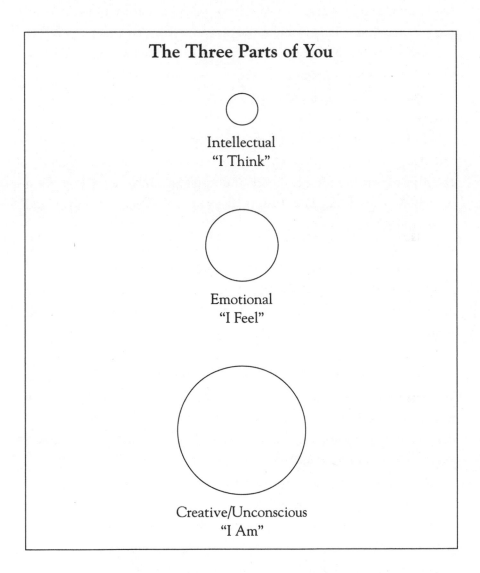

The Three Parts of You

Intellectual
"I Think"

Emotional
"I Feel"

Creative/Unconscious
"I Am"

Intellectual—"I Think"

The "I Think" dimension is the logical part of us that makes decisions and choices and solves problems.

Most training and formal education is based on presenting information. The problem with this learning model is that we consciously forget around 95 percent of everything we hear within a twenty-one-day period. Add to this problem the fact that we don't practice all that we do remember, and you have some serious flaws in the way we're taught. Remember cramming to pass a test in school, and then shortly afterward realizing that most of your knowledge, if it could be called that, had vaporized?

I'm not suggesting that having information or knowledge isn't important. It is. We must have both. However, while knowledge is essential for success, simply having it doesn't guarantee we will perform on a high level. Emotional factors like our beliefs, fears, feelings, and biases often block us.

Remember, selling is 85 percent emotional and 15 percent logical, or knowledge based. This is why most sales training fails—it teaches strategies but doesn't give salespeople a way to convert their knowledge directly into new behaviors, so that it eventually becomes second nature.

Emotional—"I Feel"

We feel different from day to day for no apparent reason, and often how we feel has nothing to do with what we intellectually know. Feelings drive many of our choices and decisions. Most of our emotions aren't even logical or understandable.

Since we know that selling is 85 percent emotional and 15 percent logical, we know that during a sale, when our logic is in conflict with our emotions, our emotions will, on average, win 85 percent of the time.

As we think about emotions, several questions arise: Where do they come from? Why do they fluctuate so much? Why don't I understand them? Why can't I control them at critical times? Why do I do or say things that I know I shouldn't?

The answers to these questions hold the key to your future sales success.

Creative/Unconscious—"I Am"

To understand where your emotions come from, you must learn about your creative unconscious dimension that houses your values, feelings of worth, and inner beliefs about who you are and what you're capable of producing. It's the source of the subconscious messages inside you that trigger and influence your feelings, emotions, and behaviors.

Your self-image, which is in your "I Am" dimension, was gradually formed by your responses to your life experiences. Once formed, it became powerful enough to control all of your actions, feelings, behaviors, and abilities. You literally perform consistent with who you perceive yourself to be, whether your perception is true or false.

The Cause of Human Behavior

Your "I Am" level is the part of you that sends silent information to your rational conscious mind. In it resides your Creative Mechanism that also operates as a Goal-Seeking Mechanism. Once you establish your desired goals or targets and you believe they're possible to attain, this inner mechanism goes to work to silently steer you toward them by sending you hunches, ideas, or insights that help guide you.

The cause of your overall productivity emanates from your "I Am" dimension. It acts as a silent, yet powerful, governor to regulate your achievements.

Where Your LifeScript Is Written

Each of us has a unique inner script that's been unconsciously written by our responses to our life experiences. Even before we had developed language skills, our early nurturing influenced it. The love we saw, or didn't see, shown by our parents, our adult role models we grow up with, influenced it. Our perception of how well we've performed in life influences it. A picture of who we are and what we're capable of achieving is stamped into our unconscious inner programming. This LifeScript powerfully influences our sales.

The good news is that you can change this LifeScript within you—if, of course, you want to do it. And, when you change it, your external life circumstances will automatically change. To increase your sales and success (however you define success), you must first change yourself at your "I Am" level. This is one of the most profound lessons I've ever learned. It's the most important message of this book.

If you're up to the challenge and committed to growth, I'll show you how to rewrite your LifeScript. Each chapter will offer you active script-changing strategies.

Now there's one last model I want to share with you before we get to work.

Understanding Different Behavior Styles

Anyone who's ever sold anything knows that people are different. They *think, act, make decisions, want information,* and *listen* differently. When we understand how different people want to communicate and make purchases, we achieve quicker, stronger rapport. Our ideas are accepted more quickly, we achieve an emotional synch with people, and they feel better about us.

Great communicators are able to recognize the different behavior styles of people and adapt to them.

Behavior-style descriptions aren't new. In fact, they've been around for centuries, since the days of Hippocrates, circa 400 B.C. Since then, people have designed any number of different terminologies to talk about behaviors—mostly psychological ones. But I noticed years ago that most salespeople don't remember psychological terms. Since I'm constantly looking for ways to help *salespeople* better understand their customers' needs, I wanted to design a behavior styles model to help salespeople learn how to intuitively adjust to different styles.

My associates and I listened to how hundreds of people described other people, looking for the most simple, *recognizable* terms.

The results of our observations can be seen in the following graph:

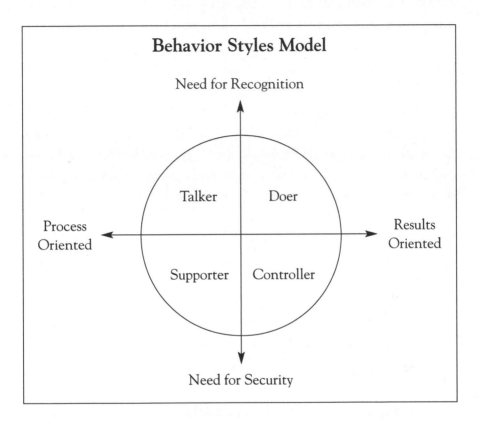

Talkers are outgoing, friendly, affable people. They like people and are colorful and fun to be with. They're easy to approach and talk to. They buy from people they like. They often find making decisions difficult because they don't like to reject or disappoint people. They need social approval and acceptance, and their greatest fear is the loss of it.

Doers are bottom-line, get-it-done people. They're pressed-for-time, action-oriented, decisive people who want to deal with the "top person." They make quick decisions once they think they have a grasp of the facts. They crave respect for their achievements. Their greatest fear is the loss of power.

Controllers are reserved and distant. They're logical and unemotional. They want facts and accurate information, and aren't swayed by your enthusiasm and personality—they may even be turned off by it. They're very analytical and well organized and will make decisions only after carefully digesting all the facts and data. Their greatest fear is being wrong.

Supporters are easygoing, steady, dependable, and loyal. They want to go slow and get a lot of information. They're detail-minded and don't make quick decisions. They usually prefer to work in the background rather than take center stage. They're team players. They need sameness, predictability, and security. Their greatest fear is running risks.

As you review this model and the description of each style, please remember the following important points and you'll understand the model more completely:

1. No style should be considered better than another.
2. People are generally combinations of two styles, with one being dominant, the other secondary.
3. Usually the combinations are of contiguous styles. For example, a person could be a Talker/Doer or a Doer/Talker, a Doer/Controller or a Controller/Doer, etc.
4. More complex people are often combinations of three styles, with the third one consciously developed.
5. It takes a combination of all styles to make up a good team.
6. Salespeople tend to sell and communicate consistent with their natural style; consequently, they often unwittingly mismatch or miscommunicate with people of other styles.
7. Rapport is achieved faster when you change your style to match other people's styles.
8. With practice, you can identify and match others' styles unconsciously.

9.   Each style wants information presented in different ways and they naturally make decisions differently.
10.   Your customers' motivations are largely colored by their Behavior Styles.

I realize that all this is far too much to process and remember simply by reading about it. But through repetition and daily practice, you'll make it part of your natural skills.

Once you've begun to intuitively blend your style with the people with whom you're communicating, you'll be amazed how much it helps you sell more.

How to Gain the Most from This Chapter

Congratulations! You're off to an exciting, productive start in moving your sales career upward. Let me give you suggestions for developing the four traits.

For Goal Clarity
1.   Set some new goals. Write down on a card, in your planner, or on something that you'll look at each day these goals:
     a.   A monthly sales goal.
     b.   An annual sales goal.
     c.   An income goal (if appropriate).
     d.   A motivational goal—something you'll give or do for yourself when you reach your sales goal.
     e.   A family goal.
     f.   A personal goal.
2.   Put reasonable target dates for each of these goals, and begin taking daily actions to reach them.
3.   Carry this written statement with you and look at it each day. Each time you read it, visualize the rewards you'll enjoy when the goals are realized. Each time you think of

a roadblock to attaining them, consciously refocus on
the rewards.

For Improving Achievement Drive, Emotional Intelligence, Social Skills
1.   Review the self-evaluations listed in this chapter.
2.   Select one statement from each self-evaluation and write it
      as an affirmation or self-suggestion.
3.   Repeat these self-suggestions to yourself several times
      each day, until, by repetition and time lapse, you begin to
      reprogram your inner beliefs.
4.   Pick out one activity each day that you don't want to do,
      but by doing it will contribute to your sales success.
5.   Begin your day by doing a most enjoyable activity, then
      immediately perform this dreaded activity. Nothing will
      build your emotional intelligence and confidence like this.
      This puts you in control of activities, rather than allowing
      them to control you.

For Learning Behavior Styles
1.   Study and memorize the Behavior Styles model and
      descriptions.
2.   Each day, concentrate on just listening to your clients; don't
      try to identify their styles.
3.   After contact with people, look at the model again and
      quickly identify, as best you can, that person's style, as well as
      your interaction with them.
4.   Identify your own style and review how you effectively
      communicated with different people. What do you need to
      change about your style to adapt to the different styles of
      others?

Your daily practicing of these suggested actions over a period of
time will help you understand and communicate with people who act,

think, and see the world differently than you. You'll also be filling one of your clients' greatest needs—communicating the way they want to do it.

Some great salespeople do this naturally; most of us have to learn. You'll learn more and more in the chapters ahead. As you practice my suggestions, you'll be amazed at how well you relate to people.

[2]

Approach: Get People to Open Up Their Mental Gates and Let You In

---
INTEGRITY SELLING SUCCESS PRINCIPLE

People are more apt to trust and open up to you when you listen to them, care about them, and have a sincere desire to understand them.

One day I got a call from a pharmaceutical representative who was enrolled in our Integrity Selling course. She told me about the sixth call she had made on one doctor. This time, in order to practice the Approach step of our selling system, she told him, "Doctor, I'm not here to 'detail' you today. I'd like to just take a few minutes to better understand your practice, and how I can serve you better."

The doctor then spent ten minutes telling her how.

As she was leaving, he welcomed her back again and remarked, "You're one of the nicest pharmaceutical reps who's ever called on me . . . why have you never called on me before?"

What a lesson. She'd been there five times before, doing her industry's typical two-minute "detail," and he didn't even remember her.

Obviously, she'd never made it through his mental gate.

Almost the same week, another rep told me this story: She called on a doctor who'd always been very busy and preoccupied. He'd impatiently listen to her two- to three-minute product presentation, take some printed information, and allow her to leave samples. On this visit, she left all the sales material in her car. She said, "Doctor, I see that you're very busy today. If you don't mind my asking, how do you balance your life with such a busy schedule?"

The doctor thought for a moment, had her sit down in his office, and spent the next fifteen minutes telling her about his favorite hobby—wine making—and how it took his mind off his work. He then went into a closet, brought out a bottle of his wine, and gave it to her, asking her to let him know how she liked it.

Guess who was welcomed back to his office any time?

Your First Sale

The approach is the first sale you must make. An effective approach prepares people to notice you, and more important, *want* to communicate with you.

As you approach people, for the first or fifty-first time, you must consciously get them to open their mental gates and move through the barriers of preoccupations or distractions that keep them from hearing you. You may only have telephone contact with your customers, or you may have face-to-face contact. You may only have a five-minute total contact, or it may be much longer. Regardless of the amount of time you have, you must gain rapport before you'll be heard.

Even with repeat customers, each time you have contact with them, you should consciously work to get on their emotional wavelength before moving ahead with your calling objectives.

The Approach Action Guides

1. Tune the world out and people in.
2. Put them at ease and make them feel important.
3. Get them talking about themselves.
4. Hold eye contact and listen to how they feel.

As you practice these Action Guides, you'll consistently make effective approaches.

You'll get people to open their mental gates and let you in.

Tune the World Out and People In

The first step in gaining rapport with people is to prepare yourself to be customer-focused. Put aside your own concerns when you contact customers, which isn't as easy as it sounds.

Most of us have many different thoughts in our heads when we approach people. "Will I sell anything to this person?" "Why did I get so upset when I burned the toast this morning?" "Does my mother really have breast cancer?"

You break your own preoccupation by focusing on your customer. You have to retrain your thoughts. "What are their needs?" "How can I help them?" "What are they saying to me?" "Let me make sure I understand them."

Before you make contact, take a couple of minutes and write down two or three needs, wants, problems, or challenges you think a customer may have. Then write down two or three ways you can help them, or ways you can possibly create value for them. Visualize them saying to you after your contact, "You're the kind of person I'd like to do business with!" Hear them telling others how you've helped them, and recommending you.

This mental preparation can do wonders in preparing you to block out your own pressing issues and focus on the people you contact.

When you let go of your own preoccupations, people are more likely to let go of theirs.

Put Them at Ease and Make Them Feel Important

The second step in an approach is to put them at ease and make them feel important. You can best practice this by being at ease yourself. Usually, a friendly, relaxed way of approaching someone is best, because people tend to mirror your actions. For most people, there's a subconscious urge to adopt the same emotional level that you present to them. This seems to work on a deep instinctual level with a few exceptions.

When beginning your approach, usually the worst thing you can do is to immediately make a sales presentation, or begin talking about your product or service. You should always establish rapport with your customer *before* moving forward. Also, it's best not to pull out your sales material right away. Whether it's in person or over the telephone, it's usually best not to give them the feeling that you're trying to "sell them something."

When gaining rapport, be aware that your body language influences people. Watch how and where you sit. Don't get too close or crowd their space. Don't try to get too familiar or casual with people, but don't be too stiff and formal, either. Lean back and show open gestures. Don't lean in too far. Don't sit so close that they feel uncomfortable. They'll reveal this by pushing or leaning back from you. Notice where they have their guests' chairs located in relation to their desks. This tips off where they want you to sit. (All this observation is possible when you have strengthened your emotional intelligence.)

Once you've put your customers at ease, you'll want to make them feel important. You can do this by, first of all, *thinking* they're important. If you can do it sincerely, compliment them on things others have said about them, or possessions you see in their surroundings. Laugh and smile to break the tension. Your body language and tone of voice should say to people, "There's something I like about you." The same is true when you have telephone contact as well—whether the calls are incoming or outgoing.

You can develop these natural responses with practice.

Recently, I called American Airlines to get a platinum upgrade. I had gone through multiple recordings before I finally heard a very friendly voice identify herself by name and ask, "How may I help you?" I told her my flight number and asked to be upgraded. She replied, "I'd be delighted to check on that, Mr. Willingham . . . How is your day going today?"

I told her, and she responded with a cheerful "Well, I hope it continues to be a good one."

In just a couple of minutes, she had made me feel special. I sensed her cheeriness was genuine, and it added to the pleasure of my day. Did she make a sale? Yes, she did, by tuning in to my needs, making me feel special, upgrading me, and thanking me.

Get Them Talking About Themselves

People love to talk about themselves, their interests, their families, their jobs, their hobbies, and their achievements.

I learned this from an early mentor, J. Henry Thompson, a Regional Manager for Diebold, Inc., of Canton, Ohio. After making calls with me and watching me strike out with two or three purchasing agents, he said, "You know, Ron, you may want to go in and ask people questions about themselves and their interests, rather than just going in and trying to sell them something."

I've never forgotten that.

Mr. Thompson taught me a question to ask people that has been invaluable to my own selling career. The question is "What are some things that have helped you get where you are today?" I've asked this question many times in many ways.

You can rephrase the question in different ways. "How did you achieve your level of success?" "How did you become president of this bank?" "As busy as you are, how do you balance your work and personal life?" "What do you do in your spare time?" "What led you into this profession?" "How did you choose to join this organization?" There are hundreds of variations to the question.

Not long ago, I was making sales calls with one of our business associates. He told me that we were going to meet a man who was probably the second-wealthiest person in that part of the country. He thought we'd just drop in for a few minutes.

We went into a conference room and met the man—a quiet, dignified person. Fairly soon into the conversation I asked him, "How did you build such a large organization?"

It took him an hour and a half to answer my question.

He told us how he came from a poor family, starting to work in a cotton-processing mill at the age of thirteen. The mill owner was so impressed with him that he paid for his college education. After graduation, he came back to work in the mill, advanced through the ranks, and eventually owned it. Tears came into his eyes as he described, in detail, what his mentor had done for him. As we were leaving, he sincerely thanked us for coming by, and apologized for taking so much of our time. A deep rapport was established.

Over the years, I've learned that everyone has a story that they need to tell, and when I ask the right questions, and sincerely listen to the answer, I can make an emotional connection with my customer.

This emotional bonding helps begin strong, lasting relationships, which in the long run result in sales.

Hold Eye Contact and Listen to How They Feel

Once, I was making calls with another of our business associates, Larry Roberts, as we called on Mark Wright, the president of the USAA Federal Savings Bank in San Antonio, Texas. In the course of our visit, I asked him, "How did you get into banking?"

He began to tell us his story. He'd graduated from a small Baptist college in the south and went to Dallas to find a job. A friend suggested he visit a person at the Republic National Bank in Dallas, the largest bank in the state at that time.

This very senior officer of the Republic Bank agreed to see Mark because of their mutual friend's request. As the interview began, the bank officer asked about Mark's experience, only to find out that he had none in banking. He then asked about Mark's degree, only to find out that it had nothing to do with banking. When asked why he should be hired by the bank, Mark replied, "Because I'm a quick learner and I work hard." Much to Mark's surprise, he was hired to work for Republic.

Mark went on to describe the man who took a chance on him for no logical reason, and became very emotional. As he described the bank officer, I have no idea why but I suddenly asked, "Was that Bob Scott?"

"Yes," he responded, astounded.

"I knew Bob Scott," I replied.

"You did?"

"Yes. You know he was killed a couple of years ago?"

"No. How?"

"He was shot by two men who were robbing his home."

He spent the next hour talking about his respect for Bob Scott, and how much his career was opened by Bob's confidence in hiring him. It was only our first meeting, but we shared some very deep feelings about our mutual friend.

I was again reminded of the importance of listening to how people *feel* as they talk. Granted, few initial conversations achieve this level of intimacy; but any time you get people talking about themselves and their lives, emotions are expressed that help create relationship bonds. Listening to and understanding how people feel has a powerful bonding effect—when we *care* to listen. It's this bonding effect that is so key to increasing your sales. It makes people *want* to buy from you—when you're sincere and not just doing it to help make a sale.

Observing people's facial expressions, gestures, and body language helps us tune in to them on deeper-than-average levels. "But I don't have face-to-face contact with my customers," you might say. This may be true, but you can visualize eye contact with them. You might even imagine the color of their eyes, what they look like, what kind of clothes they like to wear. Even though you can't see people, just thinking about these things can help you block your own world out and help you focus more intently on them.

As you practice these four Action Guides, you'll develop stronger rapport with people and you'll fill one of the strongest needs they have—the need to be listened to, valued, heard, and understood.

Give Feedback As You Listen

As you listen to people, let them know that you hear them, value them, and understand them. You can offer feedback by nodding approval at key points they make, or giving verbal responses like "I understand," "I see what you mean," and "Yes, I agree!"

You also give feedback with your body language. Closed gestures cause others to close up. Open gestures like smiling and nodding approval cause others to be more open. Interrupting people to make your own points tends to close them up and makes rapport more difficult.

When you genuinely want to listen and understand another person, you'll exhibit the proper words and gestures. So don't think about your gestures, about whether to smile or how to position your body; rather, *want* to hear and understand, and you'll exhibit the appropriate body language.

Your Expectations Often Precede Your Realities with Others

A number of years ago, Professor Pitirim A. Sorokin of the Harvard Research Center conducted numerous experiments with students who initially felt unfriendly toward one another. When one party began to try to see the other party in a more positive light and instigated friendly behavior, the other person's behavior changed accordingly 70 to 85 percent of the time.

There's a powerful message here.

To a large degree, we have the power to determine how we'll be received by customers. By having positive expectations and behavior, we can often influence positive responses from them. As I said earlier, people have a tendency to mirror each other's attitudes and feelings. There seems to be a natural dynamic of human action; people are unconsciously compelled to return to us the same attitudes and feelings that we give them. There's a name for this phenomenon—The Law of Psychological Reciprocity.

As a salesperson who wants positive responses from people whom you contact, it's up to you to take the first step. Assume that your customer is sincere, wants to be friendly, and will enjoy your visit. Genuinely be excited about meeting customers, look for good in them, and value them by asking questions and listening.

As you do so, you'll find many people are psychologically impelled to return these same responses back to you.

You'll be surprised how often these sincere efforts will help you gain rapport with people. And it works in direct proportion to your genuine interest. Your interest in a person's values, feelings, and business must be 100 percent sincere. That's why we call it Integrity Selling.

More About Behavior Styles

Now that you know the four steps in an Approach, you can learn to apply and adapt these steps to whatever behavior style you encounter. Let's review the four basic styles:

Talkers are social types. They love people. They love to visit and socialize, have block parties, arrange family reunions, and join bowling leagues. They're easy to gain rapport with—easy to approach. After ten minutes, you'll think you've been friends for life.

They like to tell jokes. When you hear the preface "Hey, have you heard the one about . . . ," you'll know you're probably communicating with a Talker.

They enjoy chitchat. They're friendly and affable, often have a cluttered environment, and their automobile interiors usually need cleaning. They like pictures and things that bring them recognition, and are often more daring with their dress and jewelry. Their motto is "Life should be fun!"

Doers are achievers, drivers. Their objective is to get things done. They're often impatient, type A people. There's never enough time. They're competitive and energetic, and attack things that get in their way. They talk about achievement, bottom-line results, and there's often a free-floating hostility against anyone or anything that tries to slow them down. They hate to stand in lines, and will do it only until they figure out how to move to the head of the line.

A Doer's motto is "I don't want a forty-hour week, I want a forty-hour day!" They like you to get to the point. They're impulsive and very decisive, and they'll make quick decisions once they *think* they have a grasp of the necessary facts and information. They're often surrounded by trophies, awards, plaques—all attesting to their achievements. They exhibit and talk about goals and rewards for achievement. Often you'll see their pictures with other well-known high achievers. They're restless and have nervous mannerisms. Another motto is "Do it now!"

Supporters are stable, even-tempered people. They're content with routine, redundant jobs. They're usually never very high or very low emotionally. They're not pushed for time and are unhurried. They're usually honest and dependable. They're the first ones to come to work in the mornings and the last ones to leave in the evenings.

They aren't risk-takers, nor do they make quick decisions. They're motivated by security. They focus on doing a good job more than getting high results. They're detail-minded for the sake of doing the

details well. They like to hang on to tried-and-true methods and techniques. Their motto is "Don't rush into things."

Controllers are logical, rational people. They're highly organized
and show strong attention to detail. Their decisions are unemotional
and revolve around facts and figures. Their motto is "A place for everything and everything in its place." They're surrounded by orderliness.
They talk about methods, conditions, and functions. They file information neatly and know how to retrieve it quickly when needed. They
reveal a high degree of organization. Their desks may be loaded with
work to be done, but it's all stacked in neat piles.

Controllers make good use of their time. They show high attention to detail for the sake of efficient management. They also exhibit
low energy and emotional responsiveness. Their greatest fear is being
inaccurate or making mistakes.

How to Approach Each Style

Each "style" of customer will require a different kind of Approach, and the
amount of time you'll spend with people varies according to their style.

Look at the AID,Inc. graph and you'll notice that the Approach
step takes up a small amount of the total selling time. You'll also notice
that in the Approach step you do 20 percent of the talking and 80 percent of the listening. This is a general statement, as you may find it
more difficult to get Controllers and Supporters to do 80 percent of the
talking unless you ask the right questions. Talkers and Doers will easily
do 80 percent of the talking, because Talkers love to talk and Doers
love to dominate.

The secret, again, is knowing the right kind of questions to ask,
because each style of person wants to communicate differently. For
instance, Talkers like to answer these kinds of approach questions:

- *How have you been doing?*
- *Where are you going on vacation?*

- *Where will you spend the holidays?*
- *What do you do for recreation or hobbies?*
- *Tell me about your children (or family members).*
- *What do you enjoy most about the people you know?*

You'll find it easy to gain rapport with Talkers. Since they like people, they'll often do 95 percent of the talking . . . or more.

Doers usually don't have time for chitchat. So don't ask them unimportant, how's-the-weather questions. But be careful—you can often misread Doers and not spend enough time in approaching them. While it's true that they don't have time for idle conversation, I've found that when I ask them the right questions, they'll often take plenty of time to talk to me. The secret lies in knowing the right kind of questions to ask and knowing when they want to move on.

Here are some sample questions that I've asked Doers. Notice how they differ from questions you'd ask other styles.

- *How do you manage to get so much done?*
- *What successful people have been your mentors?*
- *What are some things that have helped you get where you are today?*
- *What does it take to be successful in your position?*
- *How are you able to juggle so many different responsibilities?*
- *What advice would you give to someone who wants to achieve your level of success?*

My experience is that these kinds of questions encourage Doers to do lots of talking. I've made many sales and developed strong, ongoing selling relationships this way.

Here are some Approach questions that you can ask Supporters.

- *How did you learn to do your work?*
- *What are some of the important functions of your job?*

- *What activities do you most enjoy doing?*
- *Why is keeping up with details so important?*
- *How do you keep everything looking so nice?*
- *How do you stay so calm and in control of yourself?*

Remember that Supporters want to talk about security and removing risks. They want to tell you why it's better to be "safe than sorry."

Controllers, you'll remember, are logical, no-nonsense people, so these types of questions are appropriate for them.

- *What's your secret for being so well organized?*
- *How do you keep up with so many facts and so much information?*
- *How are you able to lay your hands on information so quickly?*
- *What are the most important elements that keep your organization functioning?*
- *How are you able to use your time so well?*
- *What are some problem-solving techniques that work for you?*

Analyze these questions for a moment and you'll see that they tend to focus on logic and facts. Controllers like to talk about efficiency and good organization.

Again, it makes no difference whether you're making one sale to a person or if you call on the same people over and over. These suggestions will help you to approach different people successfully. It's not so important to remember the questions as to understand the principles behind the questions. Don't expect to master these ideas instantly. They take time.

I encourage you to read this chapter over and over. Begin to observe the differences in people you meet. Stop, look, and listen—*really* listen—to people.

You'll be amazed how much better you can communicate with customers as you learn more about their Behavior Styles.

Don't Try to Analyze Style in Front of People

Maybe the most important thing to remember is that when you get in front of a prospect, customer, or client, *don't* try to analyze their style. Don't even think about style when talking to someone. Doing so will prevent you from hearing what they're really saying to you.

Confused? Then keep reading.

I've found that it's best to do my homework *before* contacting people. I try to learn as much as I can about them and use what I learn to try to determine their styles. Then I structure my approach questions according to their particular style. When I'm in front of them I don't think about their behavior style, I just plug in and listen. I absorb and match their pace, tone, and attitude. I try to feel how they feel, to empathize with them. I adjust to their emotional drumbeat.

Then, *after* I call on them, I analyze the communication and what I saw in their environment. I role-play my encounter. I analyze what I did and how I could have better related to the person's style.

Rapport means getting in synch with people mentally and emotionally—thinking as they do, seeing the world as they do, and feeling like they feel.

How to Know When You've Completed the Approach Step

1. People seem comfortable and open up to you.
2. They appear ready to move on to share their needs with you.
3. They indicate that they have time to get into your interview.
4. You can get the necessary people together for a fact-finding interview.

How to Gain the Most from This Chapter

Remember that in your Approach you do 20 percent of the talking and 80 percent of the listening. Your 20 percent talking time will be spent mostly asking questions and giving verbal feedback as you listen. Your 80 percent listening time will be spent allowing people to tell you their own thoughts, interests, and ideas.

Consciously practice the four following Action Guides this week. Notice their impact on the people with whom you have contact.

1. Tune the world out and people in.
2. Put them at ease and make them feel important.
3. Get them talking about themselves.
4. Hold eye contact and listen to how they feel.

Notice how different people approach you. Carefully analyze how their attitudes, body language, eye contact, and facial expressions cause you to feel. Pay attention to your instinctive responses and reaction when around different people.

Remember, too, not to begin selling, telling, or demonstrating until you've gained rapport, until people have opened their mental gates and allowed you in.

Accomplish these Action Guides and you've made your first sale—you've gained favorable rapport with people. You've prepared them to move to the next step—the Interview.

[3]

Selling Is an Inside Job

A few years ago, I received a call from my friend Ken Anderson, who was a life insurance agency manager and one of our certified facilitators.

"Does Integrity Selling really work?" he asked.

I remembered his subtle humor and answered, "Hey, man, talk to me."

He began telling me about a young agent who was failing in the business. The young man would get to work late each morning, always with an excuse. He'd then shuffle prospect cards until lunchtime. Then, after a long lunch, he'd get back to the office for more prospect card shuffling.

One day, Ken called the young man into his office for a talk. Sitting him down, Ken said, "Let me tell you what business we're in. We're not in the business to sell life insurance or investment products; rather, we're in the business of helping people set and achieve their financial goals. Now, what this means is that we go out, gain rapport with people, and find out what financial risks they're running that we can help them eliminate.

"Most people," he went on, "don't think about the consequences of what could happen to their families or businesses in the event of certain calamities. It's our job to help them understand all this, and then help them insure against these risks—if they want help."

For an hour, Ken explained to the young agent what it meant to help people insure against serious problems and how this contrasted with just "selling life insurance."

The next morning, he called the agent in and spent ten minutes summarizing what it meant to *help people set and achieve their financial goals*. He did the same thing each day for the next month. By the end of the month, the young agent had a complete turnaround. He came to the office early in the morning, confirmed his appointments, and ran out the door as soon as people were ready to meet with him. The days weren't long enough for him to see all the people he thought he could *help*. It was a total transformation.

What happened?

At the risk of overstating the obvious, let me summarize what happened to this young agent.

1. His *view of selling* completely changed. He now saw himself *helping* people rather than *selling* them.
2. His *view of his own abilities* changed. He discovered that he had the ability to *help* people, whereas before he doubted his ability to *sell* to people.
3. This new *view of selling* was consistent with his *values*, so he was internally motivated to do the necessary activities not because he *had* to but because he now *wanted* to so he could help people.

4. His new belief, that his products gave families and business owners far greater security than the cost of them, fueled him with purpose, confidence, and conviction.

5. After focusing on helping clients enjoy greater financial security, he also discovered that as he did, he got paid more in both commissions and respect. This experience opened his eyes to a whole new level of success and prosperity.

This story leads us to an incredibly important question: "What really impacts sales success?" It also gives us a deeper understanding of how integrity influences our sales success.

Integrity. What does it mean? Integrating the *inner* with the *outer*. Consistency. What you see is what you get. Sincerity. Congruence.

What Really Impacts Sales Success?

Deep programming within your unconscious "I Am" dimension largely drives your sales success, resulting in self-confidence, will to sell, achievement drive, self-motivation, and the expectation of high success.

Contrast this with the belief of many organizations and sales managers that success in selling is the result of product or industry knowledge, and that in many cases all salespeople need to succeed is a memorized script or sales track.

This misunderstanding is often demonstrated by the type of sales training given to people. Generally, in a one-, two-, or three-day event, salespeople are taught a sales process with no follow-up or further reinforcement. Consequently, no behavior change takes place, and no results are enjoyed. In fact, the experience can be a failure when salespeople can't remember how to put into practice what they've been taught.

After observing tens of thousands of salespeople in all kinds of organizations, I believe that most never come to understand the deep dimensions within themselves that actually drive their sales success.

What a tragedy. My experience tells me that unless these powerful inner forces are harnessed, all the skill training in the world will fall short.

The Internal Beliefs in Your "I Am" *Drive* Your Sales Success

Let's begin with a basic concept: Your sales success is driven by deep unconscious beliefs found in the "I Am" dimension. These beliefs answer the following questions:

1. Who am I?
2. What level of success is possible for me to achieve?
3. What level of success do I deserve to enjoy?
4. What level of people can I sell to?
5. What level of income is it possible for me to achieve?
6. What level of income isn't possible for me to achieve?
7. What lifestyle is possible for me to enjoy?
8. What things are impossible for me to enjoy?
9. What is the line that divides what I think I'm capable of achieving and what I think I'm not capable of enjoying? Why has this line been invisibly drawn?
10. What would I like to gain or possess, but don't believe I'll ever have?

Meditate on these questions for a few days, and you'll slowly begin to understand your own mental *area of the possible*—the deep, unconscious beliefs that drive or inhibit your success.

Let me assure you—each of us has our own *area of the possible*. And our lives are lived consistent with it.

The Power of Your *Area of the Possible*

Your *area of the possible* is so powerful that it controls all of your actions, feelings, behavior, and abilities. It works in harmony with your inner creative Goal-Seeking Mechanism. The goals you reach will always be consistent with your self-imposed belief boundaries. They act like a built-in governor that freely allows you to perform up to an unconsciously predetermined level, and then shuts down soon after that level is reached.

This area of the possible is the same inner force that causes golfers who are four strokes ahead of their usual game going into the fourteenth hole to say, "I really shouldn't be playing this well." Immediately, their automatic Goal-Seeking Mechanism takes over, and they double-bogey enough to end the eighteenth hole shooting what their inner programming tells them they *should* be scoring.

I see this pattern in salespeople all the time.

I had a friend who, for over thirty years, just barely made the Million Dollar Round Table. He drove his manager nuts, because he was quite capable of earning Top of the Table honors each year. But his sales were incredibly erratic. Sometimes he had the Round Table made by early spring, only to completely shut down the rest of the year. Other years, he wouldn't work at all for months. Fall would come around and he'd hook it up and sell like crazy, and guess what? He'd barely make the Round Table again.

This happened year after year. He'd always have excuses for not selling—illness, family matters, church obligations. He had dozens of reasons why he couldn't sell all year long.

Yes, this is a bit extreme, but most of us behave this way to a certain degree. We all perform consistent with our individual *areas of the possible*.

Herbert Benson, M.D., of the Harvard Medical School, wrote about the power of our beliefs in his book *Timeless Healing*. "Your perceptions, the collection of impressions in your head, are the reality. Emotions are the natural outgrowths and representation of the brain that takes into account a full picture of the body and the mind around it."

He speaks here in terms of physical health, but the principle also applies to how your beliefs influence your selling. Your internal beliefs profoundly affect your behavior.

Chew on that idea for a while. It will give you a whole new perspective on why you behave—and sell—the way you do.

Factors That Influence You

Of course, there are many factors that influence your *area of the possible*—early-childhood development, environmental influences, beliefs handed down from parents, education, birth order, among others. Obviously, many of these factors lie outside the scope of this book, but we'll deal with a few of the major ones that affect your selling potential.

We know, for instance, that the following factors have significant influence on your sales success:

1.   Your view of Selling
2.   Your view of your Abilities
3.   Your Values
4.   Your commitment to Activities
5.   Your belief in Product

Let's put these in the form of a model to see how they influence your selling success.

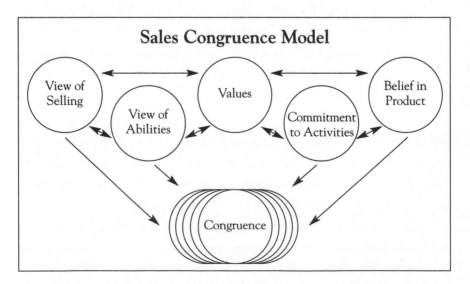

All five of these dimensions must be in congruence for you to sell to your highest potential. If you try to sell a product or service that conflicts with your inner values, or that you don't believe creates value for customers, you'll experience inner conflicts. Likewise, if you don't believe you have the abilities to do it, the same result will happen to you.

I'll define each of these dimensions, and then make some helpful points about this model.

View of Selling

View of Selling is your internal belief about what the process of selling really is. Is it something you do *to* people, or something you do *for* them? Is it a process of persuading and convincing? Or one of identifying wants or needs to be filled?

Interview ten people and ask them what they think of when they hear the words *sales* or *salesman*, and most will respond negatively. What does this tell you?

I define selling as a process of identifying and filling people's wants or needs, and creating value for them. It's a mutual win-win activity, where both sides benefit from the transaction.

This differs a lot from the typical definition that sales is about talking people into buying what we're selling.

View of Abilities

View of Abilities is your internal belief about *who* you are, *how* capable you are, and *what* levels of success you *deserve* to enjoy. We all have our own internal set of beliefs about what's possible for us to achieve. This unconscious programming then causes our inner Goal-Seeking Mechanism to steer us to those goals we believe we should be achieving. Our unconscious beliefs are so powerful that they blind us to opportunities, results, and goals that are outside our current mental paradigms.

Simply put—if we don't internally believe that a higher level of sales is possible for us, we'll ignore, or not even recognize, opportunities that would surely take us to these higher sales levels. We'll often uncon-sciously set out to prove the goal is impossible.

To bring this concept more down to earth, drive through neighbor-hoods where homes are three or four times the price of your current home. Ask yourself, "Why aren't I living in one of these?" What answers do you get? Chances are if you're honest, you'll say something like: "I could never earn enough money to buy and maintain one of these houses."

Many people also consciously or unconsciously say, "I don't think I can do what it takes to sell." In this case, they may have two distorted beliefs:

1. A negative view of what selling is.
2. A limited view of their own abilities.

But when people understand the AID,Inc. customer-focused sales process, they smile and say, "Oh, I can do that!" The gap between their view of selling and their view of their own abilities begins to close, and as it does they develop greater self-confidence and sell more.

One of the fundamentals of success in selling is being able to say, "Yes, I believe I can do what it takes to sell."

Values

Values are the rules or internal guidelines by which you live your life. They determine the boundaries of your behavior—they define what you will do and what you won't do—what your appropriate life responses are, and what they're not.

Often, salespeople are asked to do selling activities that conflict with their values. Years ago, our organization worked with auto dealers, most of whom were upstanding, honest businesspeople. There were a few, though, who played manipulative games with customers. Sales-people were taught to "lowball" customers by quoting them a low price, and then tell them that they'd have to get their manager's approval. The manager would then "bump" the price back up, and the negotiation games would begin. All kinds of tricks and gimmicks were used to get as much gross profit as possible.

Salespeople with strong values couldn't handle the stress of this type of selling. Because of the emotional conflicts this stress created, we saw a high incidence of alcoholism, substance abuse, low sales performance, and job jumping.

When people are expected to act in ways that conflict with their values, internal stress is created. But when they perform consistent with their values, they perform with energy and confidence, and both salespeople and customers feel good about the transaction.

Commitment to Activities

Commitment to Activities means performing the necessary activities that must be done in order to successfully sell. This may include prospecting or precontact, contact, presentation, or follow-up activities.

Many salespeople often say, "I love to sell; I hate to follow up." Most highly social salespeople dislike doing activities, and that reluctance usually creates problems for them, like allowing details to go undone. On the other hand, salespeople who like doing activities usually aren't focused enough on results.

Many managers manage by stressing the importance of activities, like making so many calls or contacts. While these are necessary, they don't build high producers, because most salespeople often unconsciously do the required activities and then shut down.

But goal-driven salespeople, who have a healthy view of selling, who believe they have the abilities to sell successfully, and whose beliefs are consistent with their values, want to do the necessary activities.

Belief in Product

Belief in Product occurs when salespeople believe that what they are selling gives customers value that exceeds the cost. As this belief is internalized, it becomes a conviction that then motivates them to create as much value for customers as they can.

To the extent salespeople have the desire to give extra value to customers, they become energized. This then motivates them to higher and higher sales success. A sense of integrity, or authenticity, is then subliminally communicated to customers. Trust develops. Salespeople sell more. Customers are happier and more loyal.

There's always a silent, powerful force at work when salespeople believe the value they create outweighs the prices they charge. This attitude is communicated unconsciously—giving power to salespeople and confidence to customers.

Understanding the Model

Flip back and look at the Sales Congruence Model and consider the following points:

1. Conflicts or low levels of sales result wherever gaps occur between the dimensions.
2. The wider the gap, the more salespeople experience internal stress.
3. Conflicts or stress cause mental and emotional blocks that inhibit sales success.
4. As conflicts are reduced, sales, personal confidence, and communication increase.
5. Bringing dimensions into congruence is a *behavioral* issue, not an *intellectual* learning process.
6. The dimensions come together only when positive actions, attitudes, and values are practiced in your everyday selling activities.

Bringing These Dimensions into Congruence

As you understand this model, and the definitions of each of the five dimensions, you'll be frustrated until you know *how* to bring them into congruence, and until you *believe* it will work for you. So let's think about some specific actions that will help you bring them into congruence.

View of Selling

1. Analyze the actions and behaviors of salespeople whom you continue to purchase from and enjoy the most.
2. Analyze the actions and behaviors of salespeople who turn you off and cause you to think, "I would not want to buy from this person."
3. Ask a few decision makers, "Why do you continue to buy from salespeople whom you trust?"
4. Attempt to thoroughly understand people's wants, needs, problems, or desired solutions before making presentations or recommendations.
5. Try to see yourself as a professional who diagnoses problems before recommending treatments.

View of Abilities

1. Carefully analyze the actual skills you must have to find out people's needs and offer them solutions.
2. Ask professionals who are truly needs-focused to tell you what skills, attitudes, or behaviors they've developed that help them sell well.
3. Study the AID,Inc. model and keep telling yourself that you can do it and will feel good doing it.
4. Take an aptitude or other personal-skills assessment test to discover what natural skills you have and what others must be developed.
5. Read and reread this book, which is geared toward helping you discover that you do have the abilities to do customer needs-focused selling.

Values

1. Decide what you'll say, or not say, in order to make a sale.
2. Ask successful, wise people why they trust certain other people. What qualities do they mention?
3. Think back upon people who only wanted to sell you something, and compare their behavior to that of others who were truly interested in helping you get the right solution to your problem.
4. Do the right thing because it's the right thing to do.
5. Reflect back on times when you did the right thing for people and how good you felt doing it.

Commitment to Activities

1. Focus on the reward you'll enjoy whenever you dread doing an activity.
2. Analyze why you do or don't like to do certain activities.
3. Enlist the help of others with some activities.
4. Place a financial or other measurable payoff for doing each activity.
5. Make a list of activities that you enjoy the least, and select one to focus on each day. Do this process daily.

Belief in Product

1. Focus on the value you give customers that exceeds what they pay you.
2. Allow yourself to enjoy the confidence you get by giving extra value to others.
3. Attempt to quantify what the extra value you give to customers is actually worth to them in money, time, or other measurable ways.

4.   Tell yourself that you have an obligation to serve as many people as you can because you can contribute value to them.

5.   Remind yourself that when you give extra value to customers, you'll be rewarded for doing so.

How to Incorporate These Ideas into Your Everyday Selling Behaviors

Reading the preceding twenty-five suggestions will do you little good until you develop them into your everyday habits and behaviors. Here's a way to begin: Pick out one action to practice from each of the five dimensions. Write these on a note card and carry them with you each day as a reminder to apply them. Look for ways to apply them, and at the end of each day, evaluate your performance.

As you do this, reflect on how you applied the suggestions. Give yourself a pat on the back for your successful performance. Then think about how you might have done them in the past. This comparison will help you learn.

Continue this process, and in time you'll bring these dimensions into congruence.

How to Gain the Most from This Chapter

Read this chapter several times with a pen or highlighter in hand. Make notes in the margins of the pages and highlight important points.

Go back and reflect on the ten questions I asked early in this chapter under the subtitle "The Internal Beliefs in Your 'I Am' Drive Your Sales Success." Meditate on them. Analyze why you answer them as you do. Begin to clarify your own *area of the possible*. Understand how your current level of sales success is consistent with your beliefs about what's possible for you. Study the Sales Congruence Model and my definitions of each dimension. Look for connections and possible conflicts between these dimensions. Pick out one action from each of the five dimensions and practice them each day. Write the actions on a card or someplace where you'll see it each day as a reminder to practice them in your daily selling activities.

Remember . . . your old habits or perceptions took a long time to develop, so it will take some time to learn new ones to replace them. Be patient and rest assured that with daily practice, my suggestions will soon pay off. In time, you'll discover that the new growth and confidence have spilled over into your sales and your life.

Selling is an inside job. The more you grow on the inside, the more your skills, behaviors, and sales will grow on the outside.

[4]

Interview: Find Out People's Needs So You Can Offer Solutions

> INTEGRITY SELLING SUCCESS PRINCIPLE
>
> The art of persuasion is paradoxical. The more we attempt
> to persuade people, the more they tend to resist us.
> But the more we attempt to understand them and create value
> for them, the more they tend to persuade themselves.

This chapter may completely change your concept of selling if you've been led to believe that selling means convincing or persuading people to buy your product or service. It will also benefit you if you've been product- or transaction-focused in your selling style.

If you're a top professional, though, who already sees selling as a win-win partnership, this chapter will introduce you to a process designed to help you understand *why* you've been successful. By knowing *why*, you'll be able to reach even higher levels of success.

The interview is the single most important step of the AID,Inc. system. It's the heart of customer needs-focused selling. It's such an important step that you can learn about it over and over, and yet continually discover there is more to learn. I designed the system a number of years ago, and I'm still learning deeper ways of applying it.

How to Transition from Approach to Interview

After gaining rapport with people, and when you sense that it's time to move on because of their positive responses, here's a transitioning statement you can make:

> *I'm not sure that what I have is the best solution for you or not. I can't know until I understand your needs, wants, problems, challenges, or goals. So, if you don't mind, I'd like to ask you a few questions and get some information, so that I'll know if what I have is right for you.*

You can rephrase this a number of ways. This honest statement can cause your customers to trust you; unfold their arms, physically and emotionally; and allow you into their mental space.

Interviewing Is the Heart of Customer-Focused Selling

In order to understand the Interview step—successfully interviewing your customers—let me contrast it with some commonly used sales strategies.

1. A *product focus* is where salespeople spend most of their time showing and talking about their product or service, its features, advantages, and benefits. Their objective is for people to *understand* their product or service so that they'll want to buy it.
2. A *transaction focus* is used by salespeople whose main goal is to get people to say "yes" and buy whatever they're selling. Their objective is to make a sale, whatever it takes.

3.   A *customer-needs focus* is where salespeople go through a discovery process to determine if customers have needs, wants, problems, or objectives they want filled, satisfied, or solved. Their objective is to establish a need before initiating any selling activity.

Which Focus Is Yours?

One way to discover your central sales focus is to think back about how you spend your time when talking to customers.

Do you spend most of your time in the first half of your contact talking about your product or service? Or do you spend most of the time asking questions that focus on their needs, spending at least 80 percent of the time listening?

In your typical selling situations, who does most of the talking? In an effective Interview step, you should do 20 percent of the talking, and your customers 80 percent. When you talk it is mostly in the form of questions and paraphrasing back to customers what they tell you to make sure you understand them.

How many people have ever sold things to you this way?

How did you feel when they did?

Most of your time in a needs-focused sales process is spent finding out if people have needs that you can fill. No solutions are offered until a person's wants or needs have been admitted. Paradoxically, when people begin to sell this way, we usually see a 15 percent to 30 percent increase in their sales.

With a customer-needs focus you explore, ask questions, and get feedback. You make no attempt to sell anything until the following steps have been accomplished:

1.   People admit needs, wants, problems, or objectives they want filled, satisfied, or solved.
2.   They agree that not only do they have needs, but they are open to solutions.

3. They agree to talk to you about a solution.
4. They confirm that they can make purchase decisions.

Often, up to half your contact time is spent achieving these four steps.

"What if people don't admit that they have needs or a desire for a solution?" you ask. Generally, if they don't agree to all four of these steps, you probably don't have a good prospect. Or they aren't the real decision makers. Or they don't have a compelling reason to take action. Or they aren't favorably disposed to buy from you.

The Interview Action Guides

These guides give you a process for doing successful interviews. When you incorporate them in your selling, you'll notice immediate increases in your closing ratios.

1. *Ask* open-ended, indirect questions that draw out wants or needs.
2. *Listen* to and paraphrase all points—write them down.
3. *Identify* dominant wants or needs and get agreement.
4. *Assure* people that you want to help them enjoy the most value.

Begin with an Attitude

Your attitude, which reveals your motivation for asking Interview questions, sets the proper stage for Integrity Selling.

Here are two different attitudes you might have:

1. I want to ask you questions that will lead you and set you up for what I want to sell you.
2. I want to ask you questions that will give me information so I can understand if you have wants or needs I can help you fill or satisfy.

One set of questions can be manipulative and leading. The other is sincere and unbiased.

When you buy from people, which attitude would you want them to have?

Ask Open-Ended, Indirect Questions That Draw Out Wants or Needs

Interviewing questions include the words "who," "what," "where," "why," "when," or "how." When your questions include these words, you'll get information about your customers' wants or needs. They're open-ended, indirect questions that get customers talking and you listening.

To help you design your own need-development questions, you might first make a list of wants or needs your customers have that you can help them fill. Once you've done this, you can design specific open-ended questions that will draw out the information.

Assume the role of a physician. Doctors don't ask, "What's your illness, and what prescription do you need to cure it?" Nor do they say, "Let me tell you about this new drug and see if I can convince you to buy it." No, they ask indirect questions about symptoms. Once they have enough information, they make a diagnosis and prescribe a cure.

You, too, can operate in the same professional way.

Before reading any further, please do the following exercise to design your own need-development questions.

Take out a sheet of paper and draw a line from top to bottom, down the middle. On the left side, list the wants or needs a person or organization might have that you can help them fill. Then, on the right side, write some questions you can ask to encourage them to give you information that explains their needs.

If you've followed my suggestion and written out your own need-development questions, you've got something that's worth pure gold. Keep using and refining them until you have a series of questions that pop into your mind whenever the situation calls for it.

Remember, don't directly ask your customers what their wants or needs are—you probably won't get true information. Instead, ask them indirect questions that get them giving you valuable information. Once you've received the information, you're in a position to professionally determine what their wants and needs are. Here's a good point to remember: Don't ask your customers what they want to buy, but find out their needs, and then recommend what would be their best buy!

You may know, or think you know, what your customers' wants or needs are. And since you think you know, you're itching to get on with selling or demonstrating. This is a typical response of Doers, and eight times out of ten they move to a product or service presentation much too quickly.

There's more to interviewing than just learning a customer's wants or needs. Your main purpose is for your prospects to *admit* their wants or needs, as well as a desire for a solution. In doing this, they clarify and define their own problems and often develop an inner tension for solutions.

Stop a moment, reread, and think about this last statement. It's very important. The more your customers talk, and the more you listen, the more they'll sell themselves. You'll understand this paradox more as you learn and apply more suggestions in this chapter.

As you do the Interview process, your customers will trust you more, and see you as a professional who sincerely wants to help them enjoy the best solution.

Listen to and Paraphrase All Points— Write Them Down

As your customers talk about their wants or needs, occasionally paraphrase what they say. For example, if a person said, "We have four children, so we're looking for a minivan," your paraphrase might be "I understand how a minivan would give you plenty of room for your four children!"

Besides proving to your client that you listened, paraphrasing also lets you mention a benefit that corresponds to their expressed need. "Plenty of room" is a natural benefit statement for "four children and a minivan." When you paraphrase, you let them know that you understand them and that what they said was important.

Paraphrasing also helps your customers further clarify their needs in their own mind, and it's a terrific way to deepen rapport and trust.

You'll want to also take notes while your customers speak; it heightens your professionalism and shows that you're interested and that you want to be helpful.

Identify Dominant Wants or Needs and Get Agreement

As you ask interview questions, you'll want to weigh each response and determine the dominant wants or needs of your customers. *What does the customer want to solve, satisfy, or achieve? How will she benefit from the solution I offer? What's her level of interest? How urgent is it that she make a decision?*

Watch your customers' body language, eyes, and responses. They'll give you clues as to which of their expressed needs are most valuable to them. After you feel you've asked enough questions and have enough information to determine their wants or needs, begin to prioritize.

To prioritize their needs, simply ask, "If I understand you correctly, you're saying that your most important needs are to have a vehicle large enough for your children as well as one to take on camping trips to the mountains. Am I right?"

Now, at this stage in the interview, it's easy to assume that you know their needs and thus move on to offer them solutions or recommendations. But it's usually premature to do this until:

1. They've admitted their dominant needs or wants.
2. They've admitted a desire for a solution.

3. They're willing to talk to you about a solution.
4. They have a sense of urgency in seeking a solution.

Achieving these four objectives elevates you to the role of a sales counselor rather than someone who's just trying to make a sale. It sets you apart from salespeople who don't really care what customers buy as long as they buy something. With this level of professionalism, you'll stand out from most of the other salespeople they'll encounter.

You'll often assume these four interviewing objectives have been reached only to discover later that they haven't. So be careful to achieve these four milestones before moving to a presentation.

Assure People That You Want to Help Them Enjoy the Most Value

Once you've achieved these previous four interviewing objectives, your focus will be on helping them satisfy their wants or needs—if you're convinced that your solution is the best one for them.

"But what if my product or service doesn't offer the best solution for them?" you may ask. Selling with integrity is telling them the truth, and often the *truth* is that what you sell isn't the best solution for them.

With Integrity Selling courses in over sixty-five nations, we often hear of participants dealing in this level of honesty. And guess what? In almost all cases, they're the most successful ones. People respect them, trust them, and somehow this comes back around to benefit them.

When you're convinced that you can successfully give customers the solutions they want, you'll be very convincing in your presentation.

Before moving to your presentation, you'll want to take a moment, repeat your understanding of their admitted needs, and say, "From this point on, my objective will be to help you fill these needs and enjoy the most value possible."

When you genuinely want to help customers enjoy the most value, they'll usually sense your genuine interest in them. When you're sincere, people just seem to pick it up.

More About Crafting Questions

I remember when I first put the AID,Inc. selling system together. As I had papers out on my desk, a friend came in. He was a highly refined, intelligent person who'd been very successful and had earned many millions of dollars.

"What are you working on?" he asked.

"A new sales system."

"New?" he asked curiously. "What is it, and how is it new?"

"It's a simple, systematic, more scientific approach to selling. It's a six-step system that helps people better understand the sales process. The system shows them where they are with a customer and what to do next. It gives them a track to run on."

"That's interesting. Tell me more."

"Well, I call it need-fulfillment selling. It's a different philosophy in that it puts the salesperson in an interviewing or consultative role."

"A consultative role?"

"Yes. The steps are, first, to gain rapport with customers. Next, through the use of need-development questions, find out what their wants or needs are.

"What makes this different from conventional sales methods is that the customer is immediately drawn into an interactive process. The customer does most of the talking—the salesperson mostly asks questions and listens. But the salesperson remains in control."

"I see," he remarked, displaying little amazement at my new earth-shaking discovery.

I could see the wheels spinning in his head.

"I've sold that way for years," he said.

"You have?"

"Yes."

"How?"

"Well, for instance, remember back when the Strategic Air Command Wing moved into the air base here?"

"Yeah."

"Well, they were going to build several hundred new homes for the Air Force personnel who were moving into town. I was in the home-building business then.

"Homebuilders were invited up to Rapid City, South Dakota, to set up shop and sell homes. We all had space in a large hangar there. I sold around fifty homes in one week! Right on the spot. Sight unseen. Want to know how I did it?"

"Sure."

"Well, I had eight different floor plans I could build. The usual way to sell would have been to have beautiful pictures and floor-plan layouts blown up and displayed. This way people could walk around and look at them and see what was available. But I didn't do it the usual way.

"I set up a card table. I sat behind it with two chairs in front of it. Beside me was a sample case filled with pictures and layouts of the different designs I built.

"When people came up, I'd introduce myself and ask them to sit down. I'd spend a few moments getting acquainted.

"I'd ask their names, where they'd lived, how many children they had—questions like that. As they talked, I'd write the information on a pad. I'd make notes of the children's names, ages, and gender.

"I wouldn't ask them what kind of home they wanted—I wouldn't ask them direct questions like that. I'd ask them indirect questions such as: *How often do you entertain? How many people at a time? How many cars do you own? How often do you have overnight guests?* Then I'd ask them questions such as: *What do you like most about your present home? What do you like least about it? Do you like a central entry hall? Do you like a U-shaped kitchen?* Sometimes I'd ask, *If you could describe the perfect home for you, what would it be?*

"As they answered these questions," he went on, "I'd make notes. Then, when I felt I had enough information about their needs, I'd reach into my briefcase and pull out the one plan that I felt would best suit their needs.

"And you know what?" he asked, looking at me and pausing to make me wait for his answer—obviously pleased with the point he was about to make.

He leaned forward, looked into my eyes, tapped his index finger on my desk, and said, "Out of the fifty or so homes I sold that week, every-one except two people bought the plan I showed!"

My friend's need-development questions, although seemingly spontaneous and conversational, were, in reality, well crafted. That's how good questions work. Your questions can, depending on what you sell, find out different kinds of information. Here are a few:

1.   Problems they want to solve
2.   Solutions they're seeking
3.   Quantities they need
4.   Who's involved in making a decision
5.   What they want to happen that isn't now happening
6.   What their awareness is of new products or solutions
7.   Goals they want to reach
8.   Risks they want to eliminate
9.   Their personal agendas
10.   Their degree of interest
11.   Their sense of urgency
12.   Their decision criteria

Ask Different Questions with Different Behavior Styles

You've now created a terrific list of open-ended, need-development questions. But you have to pick and choose which ones you'll use, depending on the communication style of your customer.

When selling, Talkers often respond to these questions:

- *Who will be involved in using the product or service?*
- *What do other people like, or dislike, about the product or service they're currently using?*
- *How will morale or other people's happiness be influenced?*
- *Who else will be involved in the final decision?*
- *How do you feel about what I'm offering?*

A Talker may purchase a computer because it makes another employee happy, or because it causes someone to like him or her better. They may buy from you because they like you, or because you have lunch or coffee with them. The need for recognition strongly influences them. They also need to please others—even you, the seller.

Here are some types of questions to ask Doers in your interview. Notice the common thread that runs through them:

- *What do you want to accomplish?*
- *What do you want to happen that isn't now happening?*
- *What can you do to save you time?*
- *How important is it that you get more accomplished?*
- *What problems do you have that I can help you solve?*

Doers don't demand a lot of details, so you need to take care of as many of them as possible. Since their main concern is getting results, you want to talk in terms of results.

Doers have a high need for recognition, but not the same kind of recognition as Talkers. Talkers want you to like them because of their need for social approval. Doers want you to respect them because of their achievements. Often they don't really care whether you like them or not. They do want you to respect them and admire their success.

Controllers are interested in facts, logical processes, organization, good management, efficiency, and overall smooth functioning. They are unemotionally motivated by logic, so you might ask them:

- *What return on investment are you looking for?*
- *What would help your organization run more efficiently?*
- *What risks do you want to avoid?*
- *How do you make decisions?*
- *How do you manage your functions, jobs, or yourself so efficiently?*

Don't expect Controllers to spend a lot of time visiting. They want to move on. They're interested in saving time, not establishing relationships. Since they're fact- or logic-oriented, you must be fact- and logic-oriented when you ask questions and when you answer them. Your emotional responsiveness must match theirs—cool and controlled.

Supporters are stable, dependable people. They often want to talk about stable, dependable, things. They feel comfortable when *you're* stable and dependable, and this causes them to trust you. You don't need to hurry your interview with Supporters. If they think seeing you is important, they'll take plenty of time. Ask them questions like:

- *What would help you do your job better?*
- *What risks can I help you avoid?*
- *What details do you want explained?*
- *What's worked well for you in the past?*
- *Would you please help me understand how your processes work?*

Take a moment and reread these types of Interview questions that you can ask different styles of buyers. Notice their differences and the principles of communication involved. This will help you remember that not everyone thinks, acts, moves, sees the world, or makes decisions like you do.

How to Know When You've Completed the Interview Step

1. People admit a want or need that they want filled or satisfied.
2. They're willing to talk to you about a solution.
3. You've gathered enough information to recommend a solution.
4. You've identified the decision makers.

How to Gain the Most from This Chapter

I have a confession to make. I have never done the interview step as well as I'd like. In fact, the more I learn, and the more skilled I become in doing it, the more I learn that I need to learn more about it.

So there . . . I've blown my expert cover!

I'm constantly analyzing and thinking about how I can improve my interviewing skills. Every serious student of Integrity Selling tells me the same thing.

Please read and reread this chapter with a pen or highlighter in your hand, marking important points. Study and apply the concepts that I've shared.

Here's an exercise that will help you improve your interviewing skills. Pick out a specific customer and write down:

1. His possible needs, wants, problems, objectives, or goals.
2. Specific open-ended questions you can ask him to get information that indirectly tells you his needs.
3. What you might need to understand about this person's behavior style in order to completely understand him.

As you learn more about the AID,Inc. system, you'll become aware of even more information you'll need to get from your interview—like who else will be involved in the decision, what potential objections or reasons for putting off decisions might come up, what's their sense of urgency, and what are their decision criteria.

In the next chapter, we'll dig deeper into interviewing. We'll think about how to interview groups, boards, or committees. We'll think about situations where you have diverse and even oppositional thinkers.

And finally, let me emphasize something that it took me many years to learn: Almost every time you don't close a sale, it's because you didn't do a complete interview. For as long as you sell, you'll have to continue to work on getting better at this step. As you improve, your success in selling will increase.

[5]

Developing Stronger
Interviewing Skills

The Interview step—the most important AID,Inc. step—is both simple and complex. It's simple to understand, yet complex because in order to do it well you must get to the core of people's needs, motivations, and unspoken drives.

This is why I want to spend an extra chapter on it. I'll share additional interviewing skills with you, and tell you how to interview groups, understand different people's agendas, identify decision makers and influencers, as well as offer other practical tips.

Current vs. Desired Situation Gap

Many of you will find the following process helpful in your Interview step. It gives you an overall game plan for your interviewing—both individuals and groups. It also takes you through professional steps of helping people discover their own needs by recognizing the dissonance between their current situation and the gratification they'd like to enjoy.

1.   Ask questions that get people talking about their *current situation.*
2.   Then ask questions that get them talking about their *desired situation.*
3.   Help them identify the situation gap—the difference between where they'd like to be and where they are now.
4.   Then get them talking about the *consequences* of staying where they are and not taking action.

Look at it like this:

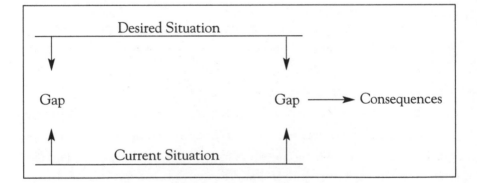

This will work for just about anything you sell—regardless of how large or small—from new cars to lawn maintenance, medical supplies to mutual funds.

I recently visited with an executive of a well-known eastern life insurance company. As he asked about our training, I suggested that we not talk about training processes; rather, I wanted to understand his organization's sales objectives. I asked him to tell me about his company's agent-retention goals (their desired situation). He told me that in two years they wanted to attain a 25 percent four-year retention, with 50 percent of agents as Million Dollar Round Table members. I then asked him what their retention currently was (their current situation), and he replied, "Industry average."

I knew this was less than 15 percent.

"What does this low rate of retention currently cost your company annually?"

"Millions and millions," he replied.

"How important is it to your senior management for this goal to be reached?"

"Well, let me put it like this," he responded. "We have to make it happen!"

By assuring him that we could help his organization reach its desired situation, I was able to position my organization as a partner in helping it reach its goals—not just one trying to sell sales training courses.

This Current vs. Desired Situation Gap can be applied to many kinds of sales. Sometimes you ask about their *current situation* first; other times you begin understanding their *desired situation*. With practice, you'll learn how to decide which to ask about first.

Everyone goes through this process whether trying to fill a simple or complex need. For example, you go to a movie and pass by the popcorn stand. Upon smelling the popcorn, you immediately consider your current vs. desired situation. If there is a gap between the two, it creates a desire that leads you to say, "If I don't buy some, I won't enjoy the movie." Or you might say, "I've just had a big meal, and I'm stuffed."

And if the negative consequences of not enjoying the popcorn seem worse than spending the money or consuming the calories, you buy it. Or, if the gap isn't there, you don't buy it.

The same basic process takes you through many buying decisions—from popcorn to automobiles. From clothing to flowers. From personal to business needs. From family to spiritual needs. Large purchases. Small purchases. Luxuries or necessities.

Often customers need an outside expert to help them move through this analysis. Great salespeople are able to counsel people through these thought sequences. They help bring clarity to people's thinking and decision-making processes.

The best, most effective salespeople know to take the process even deeper to find out a customer's fears or reasons why he or she might put off making a decision. They learn about their customer's decision process, as well as who'll be involved in it. They learn about political, personal, or relationship issues that will affect their decisions. They learn all they can about the payoff that their customers want.

Understanding Their Sense of Urgency

Asking questions that get people to define the gap between where they are and where they'd like to be will also allow you to understand their sense of urgency. This is a major objective of any interview. Rarely will people make a purchase decision unless there is a sufficient sense of urgency. Usually, two forces will determine their desire to move ahead. They are:

1.   The hope of gain.
2.   The relief of pain.

Having a "hope of gain" will include such motivators as:

1.   To look good, or boost ego.
2.   To enjoy a pleasure or reward.
3.   To earn money or increase worth.
4.   To get a promotion or advancement.

The "relief of pain" might be motivated by the desire:

1.   To eliminate risks.
2.   To keep from looking bad to others.

3. To eliminate certain economic, performance, political, or personal pressures.
4. To avoid possible unpleasant consequences.

It's the intensity of these motivations, or lack thereof, that determines a customer's sense of urgency.

Help People Understand the Consequences Created by Gaps

Skillful questions can get prospective clients talking about the consequences of not taking action. Ask them questions like "Now that I understand where you'd like to be versus where you are now, I must ask you: Are you content to stay where you now are?" Or "If what you're currently using isn't getting you the results you want, what are the consequences of not taking action?" Or you might ask, "Are you content to stay with the situation as it exists?"

After asking these or similar questions, be quiet. Wait for their responses. Read their body language. Listen to their emotions. Watch what they do with their eyes, hands, and posture. If you're working with more than one person, carefully observe how they look at each other. Chances are, you'll quickly learn a great deal about their sense of urgency.

You'll also discover who the real decision influencers are, as the others look to them for a sign of what to do.

At the appropriate time, if you truly believe you can create value for them, say something like "The real questions are: What are the disadvantages of staying where you are now, and what are the advantages of moving ahead?"

The more you ask these questions and allow the group to provide their own answers, the more you can help them make decisions.

Creating Internal Pressure

In Integrity Selling, salespeople never deliberately pressure people to buy. That would fly in the face of ethical, value-focused selling. However, customers quite often put pressure on themselves when they discover a gap between where they are now and where they'd like to be.

Once customers mentally and emotionally deal with the consequences that the gap creates, their desire for the rewards of a purchase often overpowers their resistance to change. They create their own pressure, which often moves them to make a decision. People do this when buying all kinds of things, from new clothing to groceries, when dining out, or buying life insurance.

Purchase decisions are made when the consequences of staying where we are now, versus getting to where we want to go, are unacceptable. Or when the rewards of making decisions neutralize the consequences and bring gratification. However, people's decisions aren't always logical. As salespeople, we tend to think customers always make logical decisions, but as buyers, we know that we don't.

A couple years ago, I was with my eighteen-year-old grandson, John, in Dallas. We were doing what he always likes to do—looking at cars. First, he wanted to look at Porsches and then BMWs. I was in the market for an extra car for family and guests to drive when they visited me, and was considering a Jeep Grand Cherokee. So I said, "John, let's go look at Jeeps."

"Okay," he responded, with little enthusiasm.

We looked at them, sat in the front and back seats, and opened the hatch to look at cargo space. "What do you think about me getting one of these?" I asked him.

He looked at me with what appeared to be a slight degree of pity, and said, "Well, Dado, if you can't afford a Porsche, I guess this would be okay!"

Ugghh!

We were silent for several moments. I immediately looked at my life as a total failure, wondering why I had been such a disgrace to my family. I'd always tried to be a decent person, but obviously I'd failed. How could he ever have any respect or affection for a grandfather as dorky as me?

After a week of emotional recovery, I began to think about what he said. I'd never driven one, wanted one, or really noticed them before. So I went to a Porsche dealership in Phoenix to take a look. At the dealership, Beli Merdovic, the nicest car salesman I've ever met, took me for a demonstration drive. As we were going back into his office, I thought to myself, "Okay, here you are—old as dirt, too set in your ways, and too conventional. Why don't you do something unboring and exciting for a change?"

Before Beli could finish his demonstration, I interrupted him and said, "I'll take it."

What was my pressure to buy? Hope of gain or fear of pain? Economy? Gas mileage? Recognition and acceptance? Insanity?

You guessed right. But my insanity was justified—at least to me. When my grandsons, John and Ben, not knowing that I had the car, came to see me a couple of weeks later, I picked them up at the airport in my new silver Carrera and they screamed with delight, "Wow . . . Dado . . . you're really a cool guy!" I thought, "Man, it was all worth it!"

My whole self-esteem and purpose for living were suddenly restored.

Do people always buy from you for purely logical, rational reasons? Some may, but most don't. It's human nature to buy things for mainly emotional reasons and then justify our purchases logically.

Even people who purchase commodities that are similar to the competitors' are often motivated by emotions driven by the sense of trust they share with certain salespeople or organizations.

Larger Sales Demand More Interviewing

I got a call one day from an old friend, Don Bowden, in Melbourne, Australia. "This is a name from your past," he said. It had been around fifteen years since I'd seen or talked to him.

"I'm the vice president of sales for General Motors–Holden. I know about your Integrity Selling program that you did for Chevrolet in the States, and I want it here.

"How do we get it going?" he asked.

Then he quickly injected in his typical off-the-chart Doer manner, "Oh yes, hello, how are you?"

After catching up on what we both had been doing, I told him that I had a trip planned there next month. I recommended that he get ten dealers together in Sydney and allow me to make a presentation to them.

"Okay," he replied. "I'll do it."

We discussed what would have to happen in order to enroll dealers in train-the-trainer seminars along with the project management his people would need to do.

I was careful to ask him to make the minor decision to just get ten dealers together, knowing that he didn't have enough information to make the larger decision to roll out our course to all dealers in Australia.

Did I make a sale?

What AID,Inc. Steps Did I Complete?

Think about this example and tell me what AID,Inc. steps I completed. Let me ask you these questions:

1. *Did I make a sale?* No, all the AID,Inc. steps hadn't been completed and I didn't have any money yet.
2. *Did I do the Approach?* Yes, he knew me, trusted me, and was open to my suggestions.
3. *Did I complete an Interview?* No, I had to learn much more about his current and desired situation, along with why he wanted help. I didn't know his sense of urgency, or what he perceived the consequences of not taking action were. I also had to learn who'd be involved in a decision, along with what his organization would do to support the rollout.

4. *Did I Demonstrate?* No, we would do this later with a pilot
    program for eight different dealers in order to show results
    before a larger decision was made.
5. *Did I Validate?* Partially, he knew me and about my courses
    dating back to the mid-1970s. He knew about Chevrolet's
    success, but I still had to prove results to him.
6. *Did I Negotiate?* No, not at that time. Later there was very
    little negotiation—only when, how, and where to start
    rolling out the program.
7. *Did I Close?* Yes and no. I only suggested that he make a
    small initial decision for a pilot. The longer decision was
    deferred until we had more evidence.

Although he was a very strong Doer, I knew that he'd have to
involve others in a decision about offering it to all the Holden dealers
in Australia.

Again, allow me to make the point that you don't have to go
through all the AID,Inc. steps in order to close; but your customers must
go through all of them before they'll buy. In this case, he had a need,
admitted it, knew about Integrity Selling, and knew me. So some of the
AID,Inc. steps had already been completed. But I knew that I'd have to
interview other support people, as well as dealers who were paying for
part of the program, before a sale could be consummated.

I'd have to do the AID,Inc. process with different people, in different ways, and at different times. All these parts were necessary to
complete the sale.

Interviewing to Bring Different People into a United Decision

While Don Bowden was ready to make a quick decision about buying
our program, he wasn't the one responsible for the implementation. He
had staff people who would be responsible for the details. I quickly

learned that they didn't move as fast as Don did, nor were they as eager for new projects as he was.

I had to spend a lot of time approaching and interviewing the staff and other managers to get them on board. They couldn't make the final decision, but they could sure make the road rocky if they didn't buy into the project.

And they'd only buy into the project if it filled their unique needs.

Different People's Agendas

When selling to groups, you have to be aware of different people's positions, agendas, and the ways the purchase will influence them. Failing to do this can often cause unexpected obstacles.

In Don Bowden's case, he just wanted to get results of higher sales and market penetration. The Australian managing director held him responsible for sales results, so his own success depended on moving certain sales numbers up. His midlevel managers weren't responsible for the final results, so they had different agendas. Their motivations leaned more to the side of "not rocking the boat," or "playing not to lose."

In situations like this, you can get a lot of insight by digging around with indirect questions. I wanted to know answers to the following questions:

1. Did Don's managers really want him to succeed?
2. Or did one or more secretly hope that he'd step on a land mine, look bad, and they would be in line to replace him?
3. Did the managers want to get results, or did they want to keep house, play it safe, and stay sheltered in their jobs, away from the eyes of anyone who'd want to measure what they did?
4. What was their personal relationship with Don?
5. What would be each of their perceived risks or rewards?

I learned a long time ago that everyone has his or her own agenda when purchases are considered. I always picture the following scale, and rate each person in my mind when I interview to find out different people's agendas. Usually, they'll fall somewhere between playing it safe and getting results.

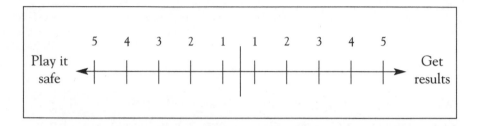

It helps to know where different people stand as they view your product or service. Is it a help or a threat to them? How important are results to them? Who can make things flow and who can clog things up?

Often, it's necessary to interview people in groups as well as individually. One of the first questions I'll ask is "Who would be involved in making a decision or implementing it, if you decide to work with me?"

Once I know this, I'll interview everyone I can to clearly understand all the different needs I must address.

Finding Out Different People's Agendas

As you already know, you'll ask different questions depending on the behavior style of the people you're interviewing. Generally, you should get two types of information from each person involved. They are:

1. What benefits they see in purchasing your product or service.
2. What risks they fear.

You can't just come out and ask these questions. You must be subtle. Here are some suggested indirect questions that might help you get to the bottom of people's feelings:

1. What have you been using?
2. How has it worked for you?
3. What are its advantages or disadvantages?
4. Who was involved in making a decision to get it?
5. What's changed in your business or life since purchasing it?
6. In looking back, would you have made the decision to buy what you now have?
7. In your opinion, is there a better solution than what your current product or service is offering?
8. If you were to change suppliers, products, or services, what would be your main considerations?
9. What do the other people involved in the decision or implementation think you should do?
10. How would keeping your old product or service or changing to a new one influence these people?

Usually, you'll find out different people's real agendas by talking to them or by asking other people. You'll probably get better information from people when you ask them one-on-one. You can also get good information about different people's agendas from internal advocates with whom you have a good relationship. But first you need to identify internal advocates.

Identifying Internal Advocates

In larger, more complex sales that involve several people, you can bet that political games will be played. Only the most naive salesperson thinks that everyone makes purely logical decisions based on the overall good of the people or organization involved.

Usually, several agendas will be swirling around, and sometimes the real decision makers won't even be aware of all of them. A reliable internal advocate can help you know the games that are being played out. An internal advocate can tell you how each person will be influenced by a purchase decision. Finally, an internal advocate can identify how you can help each person understand the value they'll enjoy if their organization purchases from you by helping you understand each personal agenda.

Do your best to identify and make friends with internal advocates and they'll supply you with insights into the people and the inner workings of their organization.

Interviewing Groups

Many salespeople make presentations to groups, committees, boards, department heads, or people with other labels.

Very often when making group-oriented presentations, the salesperson spends 90 percent of his or her time talking and presenting. I've competed against people who would go into a formal presentation with all kinds of fancy audiovisual or electronic presentations, turn the lights down low so everyone could see the screen clearly, and begin to lull these audiences into a much-needed siesta. Such a presentation might be very well prepared, professional, and state-of-the-art, but in the end it was a one-way communication with no listener involvement.

I like to go into group presentations with a simple flip chart and ask the opening question "If we are successful in this meeting, what will we have achieved?" Or "When you leave this meeting, what will you want to know?"

Then a member of my audience or I will write the responses to these questions on a flip chart or transparency. Most of the time I'll ask a participant to help me write their responses down. I do this for two reasons. First, almost anyone can write clearer than I do; and second, I want to keep eye contact with the people in the room rather than having to look away while I write their responses.

After this opening, I'll let everyone know that my agenda is not to do a routine presentation, but to thoroughly understand their needs, wants, goals, or objectives. I'll try to establish their Current vs. Desired Situation Gap.

When doing a group interview, you want to get as many people as possible to participate so that all of you work through the process together. Therefore, my questions attempt to involve all the people in the meeting.

As you're interviewing groups, you'll want to get them to quickly identify their current situation. Ask them what products or services they're currently using, how things are working, how satisfied they are. For some reason, salespeople are often reluctant to ask this. They may think that doing it could reveal that their client is completely satisfied with the situation as it is, or that it could cause negative thoughts to surface. But integrity sellers aren't afraid of the truth—all they want is what's best for their client.

After finding out the group's desired situation, ask, "What would you like to see happen that isn't now happening?"

You should spend plenty of time letting them talk and define their desired situations. Depending on the size of your sale, you'll know how much time to spend on this phase. As the group discusses the results, enjoyment, satisfaction, or specific gratification they want, they often build their own desires for something better. It's like they are selling themselves. It also gets them to focus on *what could* happen rather than on *what now is*. You help them identify the gap, and once they do, they'll unconsciously focus on the consequences of not taking action.

Harriet Butler, a highly effective and successful business associate of Integrity Systems, works with large multinational companies. She has an excellent ability to patiently get to know people and understand their different needs. She's learned to be very sensitive to different stakeholders' opinions and positions.

One of Harriet's many strengths is to use a team approach when presenting to groups, since some stakeholders will relate to one personality style and some to another. She's careful to bring in team members to work with her who will match the behavior styles of some of the decision makers.

Another reason she is so effective is that she won't recommend anything to a client unless she genuinely believes it is the best solution for them. Her values and integrity help her develop a deep and lasting trust with her customers, who turn to her again and again.

People May Have Needs
They Don't Know About

Often, you'll encounter situations where people are happy with their current situation, products, or services—not knowing that a better solution exists.

Since technology and innovation change so rapidly, new products or services are often available. In such instances, your interview will be directed toward understanding a potential client's current situation or usage. Then ask, "Are you aware of new products or services that could help you more than what you're currently using?"

In many cases, people are unaware of a problem or need until you help them discover it through your questions and advice.

Progression of Human Needs

Not only are people's purchase decisions and buying motivations largely driven by emotions, but, on a more profound level, they're a result of different levels of need in different areas of their lives. Customers can be influenced by emotions that they're not even aware of.

To help you understand this in more specific terms, I've designed a Progression of Human Needs Model.

Progression of Human Needs™

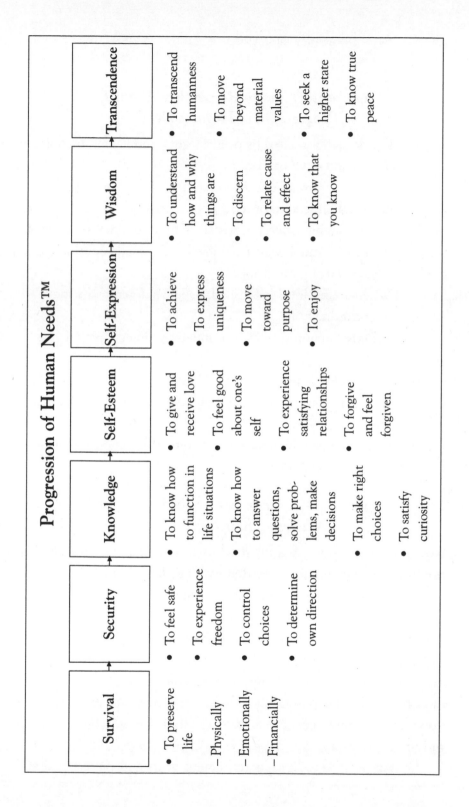

Survival	Security	Knowledge	Self-Esteem	Self-Expression	Wisdom	Transcendence
• To preserve life – Physically – Emotionally – Financially	• To feel safe • To experience freedom • To control choices • To determine own direction	• To know how to function in life situations • To know how to answer questions, solve problems, make decisions • To make right choices • To satisfy curiosity	• To give and receive love • To feel good about one's self • To experience satisfying relationships • To forgive and feel forgiven	• To achieve • To express uniqueness • To move toward purpose • To enjoy	• To understand how and why things are • To discern • To relate cause and effect • To know that you know	• To transcend humanness • To move beyond material values • To seek a higher state • To know true peace

Important Points to Remember About the Progression of Human Needs

1. People are motivated by needs, wants, and values, by hopes of gain and relief of pain.
2. Most people are primarily concerned with satisfying one need and blinded to others.
3. People can have different levels of need in different areas of their lives—the lowest need levels will usually dominate and demand greater attention.
4. When a need level is satisfied, people automatically move to the next one.
5. We miscommunicate by not understanding people's levels of need.
6. We communicate when we understand people's unique levels, and then show them how they can move to the next ones.
7. Many salespeople, not understanding this, tend to sell from their own need levels.

People Will Hear Only Solutions That Address Their Need Level

Most people are so focused on their own individual needs that they don't hear or consider anything that won't address that need.

For instance, suppose that I'm a young adult just out of college, with debt to pay, recently married, and have taken on financial responsibilities necessary to sustain my new lifestyle. My old car is worn out and needs expensive repairs, so I'm looking for a new one. I'm on a limited budget and can afford only a minimum amount for a car. My thoughts will be unconsciously focused on certain car models, and I won't consider more expensive ones. I will notice only ones that fall within my price range.

Or suppose you're in your retirement years and have saved and invested wisely throughout your life. You have an estate of $10 million. You've long forgotten any need to conserve or even earn more, and are now thinking about how you can give back. Your buying motivations will be so different from most people's that the majority of products you see advertised will have no appeal to you.

We're blinded to solutions that address needs that are outside our current paradigms or frames of reference. It's as if the products or services that don't appeal to our unique need level don't exist.

Reflect on this fact and you'll see how salespeople can miscommunicate by focusing on the features and benefits that are consistent with their own need levels, rather than their customers'.

Many salespeople have lost my business by suggesting a product that reflected their need to make a sale instead of my need to make a purchase.

People Are on Different Need Levels in Different Areas of Their Lives

This is a list of the different areas of people's lives that influence their actions and decisions:

1. Financial
2. Social
3. Family
4. Relationships
5. Work
6. Spiritual
7. Personal/Health

The Progression of Human Needs Model can help you understand people's motivations toward what they will and what they won't consider purchasing. Once you understand this, both you and the customer will gain more from the interview, whether you're selling to individuals or organizations, higher- or lower-priced products or services.

Complex? Yes, of course it is. Because all human beings and our motivations are extremely complex. You may never totally understand people's real motivations, but the fact that you try to do so will put you ahead of the game.

I learned this many years ago as a young office-equipment salesman calling on office managers and purchasing agents on a weekly or biweekly basis. I discovered when I asked the right questions, and listened, that people wanted to tell me all kinds of things about themselves and their lives. People talked to me about their children, spouses, jobs, frustrations, hobbies, and dreams. The more I listened, rather than trying to sell to them, the more I sold.

I found that when I developed strong relationships with people, they wanted to buy from me. I didn't know about the Progression of Human Needs Model then, but I intuitively knew to connect with people by listening to whatever subject they seemed to want to talk about. I stumbled into selling this way because I was reluctant to ask people to buy. What I perceived as a weakness at the time worked in my favor; I became very successful and made a lot of enduring friends.

As you become a student of this model, you'll ask questions of, listen to, and understand people in a whole new way. You'll not only listen for clues to people's need levels, but you'll improve your communication skills so people will hear what you're saying.

Stay in the Role of a Counselor

So far in your Approach and Interview steps, you've filled the role of a counselor—a professional who isn't there to *sell* people something but to *help* them determine whether or not they have a need, want, problem, or goal that you can help them satisfy.

My experience with tens of thousands of salespeople, in many cultures and organizations, is that when they adopt this *non-sales* strategy, they almost immediately sell more. This method isn't always the way ordinary salespeople think they should sell, but it is the way most people want to buy.

"I need help in closing this sale," I've been told by salespeople many times. So I ask, "Did they admit a need, or a desire for a solution? Can they make a decision? Is there a sense of urgency for them to make a decision?"

In coaching and helping people analyze why they didn't make a sale, I've found that an overwhelming number of salespeople get bogged down because they didn't really complete their Interview step.

How to Gain the Most from This Chapter

As you go about your selling this week, pay careful attention to how you do it. Analyze your selling style or strategy. Come back daily, read the following questions, and evaluate your performance.

1. Do I talk about product or service features, advantages, or benefits before people even admit a need for what I have?
2. Do I spend sufficient time asking questions that encourage people to explain to me their:
    a. Current situation?
    b. Desired situation?
    c. Gap?
    d. Consequences of not taking action?
3. Do I stay in an Interview mode until I've achieved these objectives:
    a. People admit a want or need?
    b. They admit a desire for a solution?
    c. They agree to talk to me about a solution?
    d. They can make decisions, and feel an urgency to do so?
4. Do I allow the customer's potential objections or problems to surface in my interview?
5. Do I really listen, or am I just waiting for a chance to jump in and tell them about my product or service?
6. Is my attitude "I'm not here to sell you something, I'm here

to thoroughly understand your situation, needs, wants, problems, or goals in order to see if I can help you satisfy them"?

7. Am I careful to understand the agenda of each person who's
    involved in any decision?

8. How well did I pick up on people's individual need levels as I
    interviewed them?

9. How much internal pressure upon customers did my ques-
    tions elicit?

10. How well did I ask questions that were suited to people's
    Behavior Styles?

Please read and answer these questions each day.

Doing this will lead you to the most powerful sales success strategy
you can use—successful interviewing. You'll understand people's needs
before any selling activity or presentation is initiated. You'll also position yourself as a professional who's focused on working together with
people to create the most value for them.

Paradoxically, this nonsales strategy will open up whole new vistas
of success and customer relationships for you.

[6]

Demonstrate: Show How You Can Fill Needs That People Admit Having

INTEGRITY SELLING SUCCESS PRINCIPLE
Your presentation will be much more effective when you focus on filling needs, satisfying wants, or solving problems than when you focus on your product or service features.

For several years, every six months or so, a life insurance agent would come into my office, uninvited, barely say "Hello," plop down a print-out of a special whole life plan on my desk, and say, "Hey, pal, let me show you how you can . . ."

Then, without any questions or responses from me, he'd spend the next thirty minutes explaining the features and advantages of this wonderful policy that I should have. He'd get all excited, stand up, pace around, dazzling me with his enthusiasm.

In the several years he tried to sell to me, I never bought a thing.

What AID,Inc. steps did he skip? What step did he immediately start with?

Ironically, he was a reasonably successful agent because of his persistence. I always wondered how much more successful he could have been if he had really cared about my needs rather than his need to make a sale.

A few days after one of his visits, a young copy machine rep was called in by some of our office people to explain the merits of a new copy machine to me. He'd done his homework, knew what machine we'd been using, how many copies we produced each month, etc. He briefed me on the machine that our people had decided on, and showed me a picture of it. My response was "This looks okay to me. How much is it?"

Looking straight at me, he said, "I know that the price is important to you, but let's first make sure that everyone knows what I'm recommending, and we all agree that it's the best one to fit your copy needs."

His look told me that I'd asked an inappropriate question. His response sounded logical to me, so I kept my mouth shut for a while.

He then reviewed the specifications and made sure all of us in the room understood and agreed that it was what we needed.

Having brought us all on board, he told us the price of a lease versus purchase, offering us the choice. I was so impressed with the young man's sales skills that I told him, "You're very good. I'm impressed with the professional way you handled this."

He thanked me, and I reached into my credenza and pulled out a copy of my previous *Integrity Selling* book and handed it to him.

His response was "I appreciate this, and if you don't mind I'll get you to autograph it for my boss. You see, I went to the bookstore and bought a copy, and read it before I called on you!"

It dawned on me that I probably never had a chance to say no.

Of course, we bought what he recommended. My staff would have tarred and feathered me if I hadn't said, "Okay."

When Is the Right Time to Make a Presentation?

It's time to demonstrate or present your solutions to people's problems when they've said:

1. "Yes, I have a need or want.
2. "Yes, I'm interested in a solution, and
3. "Yes, I'll talk to you about a solution.
4. "Yes, I have a sense of urgency, and can make a decision."

Before you present solutions, you must ask yourself, "Is what I have the best solution for this person's needs or wants?" If the answer is "yes," you have a professional responsibility to show and tell them how you can help. If the answer is "no," then you have a professional responsibility to tell them that what you're selling isn't the best solution for them.

This is called *integrity*. And, either way, both you and your customers win.

Demonstration Action Guides

Here are four actions to practice that will help you demonstrate your product or service most effectively:

1. Repeat the dominant wants or needs that have been admitted.
2. Show or tell how your product or service will fill their wants or needs.
3. Avoid talking about price. Make it secondary to finding out what best fills their needs.
4. Ask for their reactions, feelings, or opinions.

Everything Ties Back to Customers' Needs

In needs-focused selling, each step of AID,Inc. springs from and ties back to customer needs. Like a thread woven through a rug, the focus on finding solutions to your customers' admitted needs should be woven prominently throughout your presentation. It's in this presentation step that you have the choice to be:

1. Product- or transaction-focused, or
2. Customer needs-focused.

Observe people who attempt to sell you things and you'll see that many are product- or transaction-focused. It's a natural sales strategy, and most salespeople will sell this way unless they're trained otherwise. Not many are truly customer needs-focused, and learning how to be can give you an edge.

Repeat the Dominant Wants or Needs That Have Been Admitted

Whether you're presenting to groups or individuals, regardless of the time that has elapsed since your Interview, you should always take a moment or two and restate the customer's admitted needs, wants, and problems. Get agreement that they still want the solutions that they admitted. Your statement might be something like "As we agreed, your objective is to increase your delivery of finished goods 16 percent while keeping expenses within current limits. Is that correct?

"Also, I understand that if this could be done, it would mean a 20 percent increase in bottom-line profits, which could mean around $22 million in increased net profit. Is this pretty much what you told me?"

When you get agreement that these were the objectives they want to enjoy, you might continue, "Then I'd like to explain to you how, through this new equipment, we can help you accomplish these goals."

It's not unusual to discover that their needs have changed. If they have, you'll need to go back to an interview process.

Show or Tell How Your Product or Service Will Fill Their Wants or Needs

At the beginning of many of my own sales presentations, I remind myself, "You're not here to talk these people into buying what you're selling; you're here to help them get what they want!"

Unless I constantly remind myself of this, I catch myself trying to dominate the conversation, attempting to talk them into making a purchase decision.

Most salespeople who have strong Doer styles have the same problem, and must consciously develop the habits and skills of asking questions and listening in order to help customers work through to a win-win solution.

As Walter Carvalho, vice president of BAC Florida Bank, says, "The most important thing I learned from Integrity Selling was *not* to sell. This course taught me to listen, to recognize the needs of the person I'm working with, and to relate in a way that works *with* that person, that fulfills his or her needs."

Wouldn't you want to do business with a person like Walter?

Thomas P. Noonan, president of BAC Florida Bank, added, "Another critical contribution of Integrity Selling is that it has reminded us forcefully that not every prospect needs or wants what we have to sell." His people have saved a great deal of time by not pushing for sales when people didn't really have needs.

As a result of stopping the push for sales, the bank's sales substantially increased.

A nice irony, isn't it?

Over and over again, we find that the harder salespeople push to make sales, the less often they sell. On the other hand, when they focus on creating the most value for people, and creating a partnership with them, they sell more. In many cases, they sell a lot more.

The same principle works for sales managers who recruit salespeople.

Mike Niedert of the Principal Financial Group in Des Moines, Iowa, uses Integrity Selling when recruiting new financial-services reps. He doesn't try to talk them into joining his business; rather, he sits down with them and finds out what their career goals are. He's able to spot talent, and then spends time with prospective reps that he wants. He gets to know them, their spouses, and support people. He helps them carefully identify their career, income, and lifestyle needs. Then, once he's convinced that his recruits fit with him and his company, he tells them how he can help them reach their career goals.

He carefully explains that he will train them and work with them by focusing on their goals. He explains our Integrity Selling program and our Managing Goal Achievement course that he'll conduct for them. He even gets them started with a list of goals, showing how he will work with them to help them reach *their* goals. He then has them talk to his other agents who have reached record sales goals, earning in the upper six figures, because of Mike's coaching.

Mike has an amazing agent retention rate of close to 50 percent for four years, compared to the industry average of 14 percent. His agents hold a client persistency rate of 98 percent, and he enjoys a 35 percent increase in business each year for his unit.

Whether you're selling a product or recruiting salespeople, when you view the demonstration step as sitting down with people and focusing on how you can help solve their problems, reach their goals, fill their wants or needs, or deliver the gratification they want, you sell more and recruit better.

Don't Tell People Everything You Know About Your Product or Service

Product- or transaction-focused salespeople view a sales presentation as one where they explain every feature that their product or service has. I'll bet you experienced this the last time you bought a car. One of my worst sales experiences happened when I went into a Mercedes dealership, panting and drooling over a car on the showroom floor. A salesperson approached and without saying "Hello," or anything resembling a greeting, said, "It's got seventy pounds of paint on it!"

I thought, "Wow, how did you know that I was looking for a car with that much paint on it? You must be a psychic!" But after thinking about it for a moment, I got to wondering, "Maybe there are other cars with even more paint than this one. I probably shouldn't buy this one before I go to all the other car dealerships and look for the one with the most paint on it."

I looked at the sticker price of the car and quickly figured out that the paint was worth close to $1,200 per pound. Heck of a bargain, wouldn't you say? I mean, some other cars might cost as much as $1,215 a pound of paint.

And, if this incredible deal on paint wasn't enough to increase my lust for the car, without saying a word, but smiling like a cat that had trapped a canary, he reached in, pulled the hood release, popped it, motioned me over to look at the engine, and began talking endlessly about the exciting cubic liters of displacement of the engine.

As he went on about all the wonderful technical features, I prayed that he'd get hungry or thirsty, or need sleep, or have to go to the bathroom—anything just so he'd quit talking. I didn't dare ask what a "liter" was. I couldn't afford three more hours for him to explain.

You've probably experienced similar experiences with salespeople. Many don't know to mention only features and their corresponding benefits that appeal to people's specific admitted needs.

That's what being customer needs-focused is about!

People Have Different Reasons for Buying

Generally your product or service will be one that people:

1.   Must have, or
2.   Desire, but can live without.

A person with blocked arteries must have surgery to survive, but someone shopping for new shoes has many options.

People make two basic types of decisions: emotional or logical.

In other words, people make purchase decisions for:

1.   What it will do for them, or
2.   How it will make them look to others.

You've also learned about two kinds of reasons people buy:

1.   Ones that they tell you about.
2.   Ones that they don't tell you about.

Is what you sell necessary or discretionary? Does logic or emotion drive your customers' decisions? Do your customers actually buy your product because of how they will look to others, but give you a different reason? The more I sell, the more I'm convinced that many people believe that logic drives their purchases, when, actually, emotion does.

As you're making your presentation, you can serve your customers better by determining their strongest motivation for buying. You can begin to understand this in your Approach and Interview. You won't always know, but simply attempting to find out puts you ahead of your competition. During your presentation, however, you must ask indirect questions to help you read between the lines.

Notice people's Behavioral Styles, their environment, their personal appearance, their interests, their level of success or authority—these factors tend to give you clues as to whether a person is an emotional or logical buyer.

It's easy for salespeople to mistake customers' interests when they look only through their own eyes. Since salespeople's product or service features are benefits to them, they often mistakenly think they are to customers also. But customers buy benefits, not features. The Mercedes salesperson mistakenly thought I was interested in technical and functional features, when I was really interested in color, style, and ego satisfaction.

Stop a moment, go back, and review this section. Think about why people have bought from you in the past. Next, try to determine *why* people will buy from you in the future.

Often, knowing *why* people buy gives you much more insight into *how* to sell to them.

When Presenting to Groups

Do you present to groups or couples? If you do, then you know that different people have different interests and agendas that tend to complicate your presentations. You should identify these differences in your Interview and adjust your presentations to it.

Different people's agendas can range from seeking enjoyment to increasing profits, conserving energy to reducing risk. They can be functional or economic, esoteric or ego-focused. But you can often measure the degree of each member's motivations in your interview.

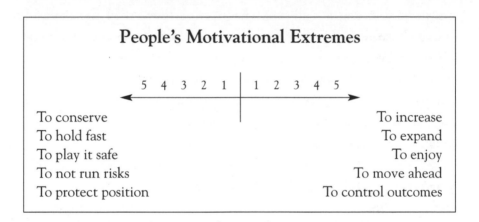

When presenting to groups or couples, such conflicting motivations often arise. If you don't discover them in your interviews, you can be in for a difficult time when you begin to present solutions. Developing an understanding of the motivation of those involved in group decisions is essential if you're selling large-ticket items. You may either interview all the people who'll impact the decision, or find an internal advocate, who understands all the players, to help you understand what everyone will or won't want. Also, you must find out what each person's stake in the game is—what are the risks and/or rewards that will occur if they buy from you?

Once you have a feel for this information, you can then tailor your presentation to the individual needs and power levels of the people. In different cases, it's necessary to outline how your recommendation will benefit each of them. This may involve several presentation sessions.

Avoid Talking About Price. Make It Secondary to Finding Out What Best Fills Their Needs

Many years ago, when I owned a retail furniture store, an old pro gave me some very good advice. He said, "The price isn't important . . . until people find what they want." He mentioned this to me when he saw customers running me all over the store as they asked the price of things they saw. After hearing his advice, I began responding to people's price questions by asking, "Is that a piece that interests you?" or "Is that what you're looking for?" before telling them the price. Often they admitted that they weren't really interested in that particular chair, or sofa, or table. So instead of talking about price, I'd go back to my interview and find out exactly what they wanted.

I never forgot the man's advice. The price isn't important until your customers find what they want or need.

When Should You Talk About Price?

Talk about price when you think people believe that the value you offer them exceeds their cost. As you've discovered, many customers bring up the issue of cost long before it's appropriate to even consider it, usually during the Approach or Interview.

Imagine a balance scale. When you put something on one side, that side goes down and the opposite side goes up. This is what happens when we consider a purchase. We weigh the cost against the value before we make a buying decision. The cost includes such things as money, time, commitment, risk, trouble, and other considerations. The value includes what it will do for customers—the specific benefits they'll enjoy. But, in the real world, people begin asking about price long before you've had time to establish the value to them.

So, what do you do?

Responding to Premature Price Questions

Let me give you a general strategy for dealing with premature price questions. It's helped many people make sales they wouldn't have otherwise enjoyed.

Let's assume that someone asks you prematurely, "How much does it cost?" Your response might be:

> *I appreciate your concern about the cost. I know that you want the best price possible . . . (Argue their case for them—tell them why they should be concerned.) . . . But before I can quote you an exact cost, there's some more information I need . . . (Then immediately ask for the information.)*

Stop and think for a moment and you'll see that this response is often true and will help you handle many premature price questions that you get. Customers usually understand the logic of your statement and realize that their price questions were premature. This can get them back on equal footing with you, and you can then move on and determine whether your recommendation is the right one for their needs.

You've essentially told them, "Let's make sure I have the best solution, and then we'll deal with any price issues." Think about this for a moment and you'll see that it isn't at all manipulative; rather, it is an honest response.

Because we get pounded with price questions so often, it's common for salespeople to assume that price is the only determinant of a purchase decision. But it's more than that. The question that determines a sale is: *Do the advantages and benefits outweigh the costs?*

Presenting to Different Behavior Styles

You will demonstrate differently to different Behavior Styles. You'll talk about different issues and results.

1. Doers—talk in terms of results, the bottom line, achievement. Keep your presentation short and abbreviated, making it clear to them that you'll take care of details and will deliver end results.
2. Talkers—talk about how they'll look to others, and how they'll enjoy owning your product or service. Show them you're a friend who cares about them.
3. Supporters—give lots of details: how things work, what to do if things go wrong. Take as much pressure off them as possible. Expect them to take more time and go slow when accepting new ideas. Don't present ideas that require too much change on their part.
4. Controllers—talk to them in logical terms. They'll show little emotion, and will not give you as much feedback as Talkers or Doers. They'll be more critical in evaluating your presentation, perhaps by demanding proof or evidence to support your claims.

Ask for Their Reactions, Feelings, or Opinions

You'll remember that the AID,Inc. chart shows you doing half of the talking in your presentation and your customers doing the other half. How do you do this? Ask questions, solicit opinions, get feedback, ask for clarification, and listen while you're presenting.

This interaction is vital in order to make the right impact during your presentation. It also proves your genuine desire to fill your customer's needs. Most important, it gets both of you involved in helping them make the best decisions.

When you really want to know what people are thinking, this inter-action becomes a very powerful form of persuasion. I'll explain further.

The Psychology of Persuasion

Many salespeople and sales managers think that persuasion happens when salespeople flood prospective customers with product features, advantages, and benefits. They tend to believe that saying the right thing to customers, or "hitting their hot buttons," will trigger a pur-chase response.

Things *can* be sold this way, but it's a hit-or-miss approach. Often customers don't feel valued because their needs aren't the main focus of the salesperson's strategy. It becomes obvious to customers that sales-people are just trying to sell them something. This usually triggers resistance from the customer in proportion to the insistence of the salesperson.

I've learned over the years that there's a much more powerful, and professional, way of making a presentation. Instead of trying to per-suade people, I attempt to understand them. My technique involves *social interaction*, a two-way communication where:

1. Information is presented by a salesperson.
2. Opinions and feedback are solicited from customers.
3. Customers' ideas, opinions, viewpoints, and questions are valued, listened to, and understood.
4. Salespeople give positive verbal and physical responses and make rewarding remarks to customers' opinions.

This four-step process should be viewed as a *value* and not just a *sales strategy*. These customer-focused activities must be consistent with your *values*; you must *value* the philosophy for it to be effective. Other-wise, there's a lack of congruence, which customers can sense in a con-scious or subliminal way.

Persuasion Occurs at the Instinctive Level

Most sales training of the past, and even the present, has been shallow and one-dimensional. It made the assumption that if you tell people about what you sell, describe its features and benefits, then the sheer logic of your offering would convince them to buy from you.

Not so!

Persuasion occurs at a very deep instinctive, rather than intellectual, level. Customers often feel, respond, and make decisions without consciously knowing why. When salespeople are sincere about listening to and understanding people, an emotional bonding takes place. The new relationship fulfills one of the deepest needs people have—the need to be valued, recognized, and understood. This bonding is enhanced when we give reinforcement to people by:

1.   Nodding approval.
2.   Leaning forward to show interest.
3.   Smiling at appropriate moments.
4.   Giving verbal approval: "I see," "I understand," etc.
5.   Asking clarifying questions: "Tell me more about that," "How did you feel when that happened?" etc.

These are five natural ways to give reinforcement, or what I call *psychological value*, to people. Psychological value is showing that we value people—*who* they are, *what* their needs are—and that we have a sincere desire to help them. It's communicated, unconsciously, from your "I Am" to your customer's "I Am" dimension. And its power is multiplied by your level of sincerity.

To help you understand more of this power, I'll explain another dynamic law of human action.

The Law of Psychological Reciprocity

I've alluded to this law in many indirect ways already, and you'll continue to learn new levels of its power for as long as you sell. Let me emphasize this dynamic law in the context of your presentations. Translated, the law means: *People tend to give us back the same feelings, attitudes, and responses that we give them.*

Kids intuitively know this; adults tend to forget it when we grow up. The law is simple: Give a big smile to ten people and you'll get a similar response from most, if not all, of them. Frown or say something unkind to people, and you'll trigger the same responses being returned to you.

So what does this mean for those of us who sell? If our central sales focus is to create value for people, we will cause people to unconsciously want to return value to us. They often discover that the best way to give value to us is to buy from us, to respect us, and refer us to other people.

Include these powerful persuasion concepts into your presentations, and you'll add power and integrity to them.

How to Know When You've Completed the Demonstration Step

1.　People understand your recommendation and believe it will fill their wants or needs.
2.　Their questions and concerns have been successfully answered.
3.　Everyone who has decision influence has been included in your presentation.
4.　You've identified any roadblocks, concerns, or apprehension they may have had about making a decision.

How to Gain the Most from This Chapter

You'll want to read this chapter through several times, underlining and making notes on the pages. Transfer these four Action Guides onto index cards or an electronic device.

1. Repeat the dominant wants or needs that have been admitted.
2. Show or tell how your product or service will fill their wants or needs.
3. Avoid talking about price. Make it secondary to finding out what best fills their needs.
4. Ask for their reactions, feelings, or opinions.

Read and review these each day. Practice them every chance you get. Evaluate your performance each time you think of it.

After each contact, stop and write your answers to the following questions:

1. How well did I present solutions to this person's admitted needs?
2. What was this person's behavior style?
3. What level of *psychological value* did I give this person?
4. When I listened to and valued this person, how did he or she return value to me?

Asking and answering these questions can help you learn the psychology of persuasion in real-life experiences. Taking time to evaluate and analyze your contacts, and making notes afterward, will give you a dynamic learning experience that you can't enjoy by just mentally trying to do it.

As you focus on understanding people's needs and giving them value, they'll usually return this value and respect to you.

As this deep, profound strengthening happens, your life will gradually change. You'll move into the rare atmosphere of high success and respect that few salespeople ever reach. You'll have more confidence, and your professional image will reveal your growth. Your expectations will increase. Your whole internal *area of the possible* will grow beyond your previous self-imposed limits. Your sales will increase. You'll discover the paradox of success and prosperity: They are a by-product of creating the greatest value for the most people—materially, emotionally, and in relationships.

Tell yourself daily that not only can you *enjoy* higher levels of success, you also *deserve* it.

[7]

Releasing Unlimited
Achievement Drive

INTEGRITY SELLING SUCCESS PRINCIPLE

**Sales power is released to the extent that your desire
for the rewards of higher goals excites, energizes, and
motivates you to learn, grow, and stretch.**

Blake Esterday, a Wake Forest University sophomore selling books
door-to-door during the summer for Nashville's Southwestern Company, understands high achievement drive.

He is expected to give at least thirty demonstrations during each
13.5-hour workday. One week, he set a goal to hit the President's Club,
which meant selling twice as much as his best week to date. Since he'd
had some great weeks already, this was quite a challenge.

He met the new week with a positive attitude. When the week was
over at 11:05 P.M. on Saturday evening, he'd worked 85.5 hours, given
253 demonstrations, and sold over $5,000 worth of books. But he was
still one sale short of reaching the President's Club.

Realizing that some people were still awake, he went to a nearby

Waffle House, trying to find someone who had children and might be a prospect to buy his books. He stayed there until 2:30 A.M. Sunday. Although he failed to make that one extra sale, he earned the honor of being the number-one first-year salesperson that week.

Blake is a great example of someone setting a goal, committing to do it, and being energized by it.

Blake's extremely high achievement drive resulted in his release of unusual levels of energy, enthusiasm, and purpose. His strong desire and commitment drove his high sales-activity level. He learned a success principle that will serve him throughout his life: Set a goal that excites you and gives you purpose. Doing so will motivate you to push through most barriers and will energize you to tackle the tough tasks.

Furthermore, Blake demonstrated the four core success factors: strong goal clarity, high achievement drive, healthy emotional intelligence, and excellent social skills.

The Beginning Point of All Achievement

All high achievement begins with strong desire—a craving for something you don't have. The level of commitment you're willing to make will reveal to you the strength of your desire, which will ultimately determine your realization of it.

Highly successful people have clearly defined goals they want to reach, and make a no-withdrawal commitment to reaching them. They aren't people who've never had problems, defeats, or roadblocks; rather, they simply haven't allowed these natural challenges to stop them.

I've been blessed with three or four major defeats in my career, times when people around me were saying "Give it up! Why fight it?" It seemed that almost no one but me believed that I could work through the problems I had and reach the goals I'd set. Yet I found that when I refused to quit, some door always seemed to open. I always found a way to work through the roadblocks.

I've interviewed many successful people, all of whom faced struggles, hardships, or roadblocks that would have stopped most people. They all agreed that anyone with a clear goal and an indomitable will to attain it eventually will discover a way to reach it. Roadblocks tend to collapse, and doors spring open when strong desire persistently knocks on them.

So my question to you is: "What do you want to happen in your future so strongly that you'll make a no-withdrawal commitment toward getting it?" In other words: "What goals are so important to you that no roadblock can stop you from reaching them?"

Take your time when answering this. In fact, you may want to meditate on your answer, or consult with a person who can give you ideas, support, or unconditional acceptance. Often, someone's acceptance, encouragement, or belief in us can help us push past barriers that might have previously stopped us.

The rest of this chapter will have practical meaning when you make a no-withdrawal commitment to reaching your goals.

Inspirational Dissatisfaction

Two of my early mentors were Napoleon Hill and W. Clement Stone. Their book *Success Through a Positive Mental Attitude* helped me change my life. Mr. Hill passed away in the early 1970s, but I had the privilege of working with Mr. Stone personally in 1980. I learned many things from him.

He taught me about *inspirational dissatisfaction*, the attitude of being genuinely thankful for what you have, while constantly striving to reach even higher goals. High achievers always want to dream loftier dreams, enjoy more of what life has to offer, and contribute more to the world than ever before.

Inspirational dissatisfaction will create a balance within you. You'll become less neurotically driven to attain more things to impress others or satisfy your ego. You'll begin to balance your natural acquisitive needs with a healthy motivation to contribute as much value to others. You'll develop a sincere desire to be your best, give the most, and enjoy the balanced rewards of success to the fullest.

In a sense, it is a matter of personal stewardship—an obligation to humbly give thanks for our rewards while using our talents to serve others.

So here's the *inspirational dissatisfaction* question: *How thankful are you for the good things in your life, and what is your level and intensity of desire to continually achieve more, contribute more, or become more?* Your answer to this question can predict your achievement drive, your will to succeed, and your will to sell.

Your Will to Sell

All of us who sell have an internal desire that I'll call a *will to sell*. Your will to sell is driven by the level of your *inspirational dissatisfaction* and is determined by how deeply you want the rewards that increased selling will give you. It's regulated by what you believe you are capable of, or how worthy you feel of enjoying higher success.

Most salespeople struggle with these beliefs because we must constantly face our fears: of the unknown, of rejection, of failure, of change, and even of sustained success. Sure, selling is fun and energizing. It can give us a runner's high. But it's not easy. Our rejections and blown sales can be devastating, and we require a strong *will* to succeed.

Every salesperson makes an emotional choice. We can either focus on the rewards of higher sales success, or we can focus on the difficulties we inevitably face when selling. This unconscious choice then drives our will to sell.

Focusing on the rewards of higher sales energizes us, while dwelling on the difficulties ahead debilitates us, both physically and emotionally. You can easily demonstrate this with a kinesiology experiment. Here's how: Ask one or two other people to hold one of their arms up parallel to the ground. Now test their arm strength by gently pressing down with your hand on their wrist.

Once you've gotten an idea of their actual arm strength, ask them to close their eyes and begin thinking of some of the difficulties they face in selling, what they don't like about it. Allow eight to ten seconds for them to think of these unpleasant things while keeping their eyes closed. Then ask them to raise their arms, and test their strength again. You'll find that they've lost almost all of their initial strength.

Next, ask them to close their eyes and to focus on the rewards they'll enjoy when they reach or exceed their sales goals. Again, allow eight to ten seconds to elapse, and check their arm strength again. You'll almost always find them to be stronger than they were at first. Focusing on the rewards they'll enjoy always adds to their natural strength. Focusing on the difficulties almost always obliterates their natural strength.

Since strength is energy, and our bodies, minds, and spirits are interconnected, it's logical to assume that our emotional strength is as weakened by focusing on difficulties as is our physical strength.

This is a powerful and eye-opening demonstration. Dozens of applications of this principle can be applied to selling.

Achievement Drive Is Emotionally Induced

Our will to sell, or achievement drive, is an emotion that's not consciously induced, but is the indirect result of what we choose to focus our minds on. This sounds so simple, yet it's quite difficult to practice at times. It's important to note that achievement drive is induced by emotions rather than logic. Pure logic can even hamper salespeople's ability to produce, by causing us to quit or avoid fighting through seemingly impossible roadblocks that only strong emotions can carry us through.

I've faced numerous obstacles where logic told me to walk away. There appeared to be plenty of proof that I was beaten; yet I was driven to push through the roadblocks and use them as motivation. In 1980, because of skyrocketing interest rates, a highly successful organization suddenly defaulted on a $600,000 payment to my firm. It was devastating, a hit that we couldn't absorb. I already owed around $100,000 to suppliers and $200,000 to my bank, and faced 21 percent interest rates. I had to lay off my entire staff of fifteen employees, keeping just one part-time assistant, and had to sell equipment for pennies on the dollar. My ability to work through all this looked bleak if not impossible.

Two or three of my advisers suggested that I file for bankruptcy, which I would never have considered. Fortunately, rather than calling my note, my banker and good friend, Dave Warren, stuck with me. I didn't know it at the time, but he personally guaranteed my note to his board and the bank examiners.

After the initial shock, I sat down and set goals to work through the financial hit in order to emerge stronger than ever.

I had two ways to earn income; one was through speaking fees, and the other was by selling training materials. I decided that my goal was to design the most result-producing sales training program that had ever been done. I was dissatisfied with all the tricks and gimmicks that sales-people were being taught, so I asked myself, "How do people like to buy things?" It seemed to me that this was the key to sales success and customer satisfaction—and the key to keeping my career and business afloat.

Because I was motivated by necessity, my creative mechanism responded by guiding me to design the AID,Inc. system that you're learning in this book. In a few years, I had designed a complete one-year Integrity Selling curriculum around this system.

Each day I pictured hundreds of salespeople using the system and selling more, earning more, and enjoying higher customer loyalty. I knew that helping organizations with Integrity Selling was my ticket out of the financial bind I was in.

I set a motivational goal to give myself a new Mercedes 450 SEL when I had the bank and all my bills paid off. It took me two years to pay two printers and four years to pay the bank. Once they were paid, I immediately paid myself on my promise and bought the Mercedes. I'd earned it.

In the years when I was working out of debt, I often traveled to Los Angeles to do a seminar. Each time, I'd arrive half a day early, rent a car, and spend time driving through Beverly Hills, looking at all the homes. I'd slowly study what made them stately or beautiful. I'd go into shops on Rodeo Drive, admiring the expensive things I couldn't afford yet. I fed their beauty to my creative mind. I analyzed them to understand the designs that made them beautiful and expensive.

Several times, I went into a Rolls-Royce dealership in California, Chicago, or New York and talked a salesperson into allowing me to sit in the backseat of one of the models. I'd inhale the smell of the British leather and wood and allow all my senses to absorb everything about the cars.

Once, at a seminar in Las Vegas, I set a goal for product sales higher than any I'd set before. When I beat it, I walked a few doors down to Neiman Marcus and bought myself an expensive Oxxford suit. I'd learned that it was very important to reward myself for hard work and goals reached.

Looking back, as tough as these times were, they were wonderful years, and I grew personally and professionally in many ways.

Setting Motivational Goals

Years before the events that would spawn AID,Inc., I'd intuitively learned to set motivational goals. You probably have too. A *motivational goal* is something you promise to give yourself when you reach your sales or income goals.

Once the motivational goal has been set, you must then focus only on the rewards you'll enjoy when you reach it, never allowing yourself to dwell on the difficulties that you might encounter. Allow these pictures to energize you, to create energy and motivate you by *pulling* rather than *pushing* you toward the object of your desires. Imagining your rewards will give you not only more energy and confidence, but also greater and higher hopes for the future. Your self-respect will also increase.

The pull of an exciting goal will take you past roadblocks faster than all the willpower in the world.

The Myth of Willpower

Logic and willpower go together, as do emotions and motivation. Many managers don't see the connection, but both logic and willpower demand rigid sales and reporting strategies. Logic will help you see how making five contacts can lead to one sale. But willpower is necessary in order to *push* us and get us going—making that first call at 8:30 A.M., telephoning until you get next week's appointments filled, etc. But willpower can stress us if we rely on it alone.

Similarly, while discipline can help us to get results, it can take us only so far in our long-term sales success. Only the *pull* of motivation for rewards serves us in the long term, causing us to soar into the big leagues of selling success.

In short, discipline and willpower are needed to get us started doing activities, but only our emotions cause us to release high achievement drive to reach our goals. It's a balance. Willpower can drain our energy, but focusing on rewards can bring it back.

Highly successful salespeople have the ability to *self-start*, and exercise a high degree of discipline and initiative. Once under way, though, they must tap into those deeper levels of emotional energy that are fueled by their deep desires to reach exciting goals. They must learn the difference between push and pull and the right time for each.

Developing Motivational Intelligence

Emotional intelligence is the ability to understand your own feelings and emotions and their impact on your behavior. *Motivational intelligence* is the self-knowledge to understand what motivates you. Select the goals or other influences that excite you and pull you toward them.

"Motivation is anything that induces action or determines choice," wrote Napoleon Hill and W. Clement Stone in their classic *Success Through a Positive Mental Attitude*. "A motive is an inner wage within an individual which incites him to action, such as an idea, emotion, desire, or impulse."

Motivation is hope, and hope is the magic power that pulls us toward future rewarding goals. Hope for a better tomorrow. Hope for specific rewards. Hope for improved skills. Hope for greater vision.

Let me ask you a few key questions:

1. What activities excite you the most?
2. What would you like to have, gain, enjoy, or possess that you don't have now but get excited just thinking about?
3. What do you want to provide for people you love that you're willing to work hard for?
4. What meaningful reward can you give yourself when you meet your weekly, monthly, quarterly, and annual sales goals?

It's important that you spend time answering these questions. They'll help you identify your unique motivators—things, results, or rewards that have pulling power for you.

Having motivational intelligence is knowing what uniquely motivates you to do the necessary actions that bring you the rewards you want. To be highly successful, you must carefully determine what excites you and motivates you, then set up those motivators that can energize you to reach any goal that's really important to you.

Certain Causes Produce Predictable Effects

Let's begin with this logical assumption: All your decisions and subsequent actions spring from a unique cause—an inner motivation. Understanding these motivations can help you take charge of your life, by allowing you to identify the necessary steps to achieving higher goals. You'll be able to answer the questions "*What* do I most want to happen in my life?" and "*Why* do I want this to happen?" and "*What* must I do to make this happen?"

To better understand this, think of the ten major motives that inspire and trigger people's voluntary choices and actions, taken from the book *Success Through a Positive Mental Attitude*:

1. The desire for self-preservation.
2. The emotion of love.
3. The emotion of fear.
4. The emotion of sex.
5. The desire for life after death.
6. The desire for freedom of body and mind.
7. The emotion of anger.
8. The emotion of hate.
9. The desire for recognition and self-expression.
10. The desire for material gain.

Reread these ten basic motives. Study them. Notice how some can lead you into creative channels, while others can drive you into destructive ends. Reflect on which have motivated you to act—in either a positive or negative way.

I've reflected on them many times since I first read Hill and Stone's book. I learn more each time I do. I challenge myself to understand why I do certain things, make certain choices, or select certain goals. What drives me? What reward am I seeking? I continue discovering deeper and more subtle motivations as the years go by.

Over the years, I discovered that my upbringing had a devastating influence on my self-esteem. I was consistently beaten down, criticized, and ridiculed by my father. Never in the forty-nine years that he and I both lived did I hear him compliment me. Even when I was no longer under his thumb, the effects of his emotional abuse stayed with me.

I always wanted to be a salesperson, yet as I began my sales career after college, I experienced severe call-reluctance. I discovered that much of my motivation for success was simply to gain the approval of people. Once I knew that purchasing agents wanted to see me and buy from me, I had all the confidence in the world. But before I was assured of this acceptance, I had an enormous fear of rejection.

In time, I discovered that my fear of rejection, along with my need for acceptance, drove many of my actions. When I thought that I'd be accepted, I had confidence and was very socially engaging. When I perceived that I might not be accepted, I experienced devastating fear. I also had a deep desire to achieve, which added to the emotional conflict it took me years to understand and work through.

Ironically, the conflicting emotions that once held me back eventually helped me develop the AID,Inc. system of selling.

Because of my need for acceptance from people, I failed at the heavy-handed selling strategies that I'd been taught. So I invented a way of selling that I could do successfully. I've learned that it's the best and most effective way to sell, and so have my customers.

Motivators Can Be Positive or Negative

Your deep, inner desires, or motives, can be either constructive or destructive, depending on how consistent they are with your values. Positive emotions of love can be destructive if they're narcissistically self-directed. Negative emotions, such as anger, can be justified if directed toward an evil. Fear can positively help us to protect our lives, or it can negatively keep us in an emotional prison.

The difference between positive and negative motivators lies in your values. Allowing positive values to guide your decisions, choices, actions, and behaviors will help you to transform your motives into constructive influences.

Remember the Sales Congruence Model that I shared with you earlier in this book? On the next page, take a fresh look at it, as it relates to releasing achievement drive. First, understand that achievement drive will be released or bottled up depending on the congruence of these five dimensions.

The reason that I mention this model again is that it can be understood on several levels. So please don't skip by it, thinking that you already know it. You can always drill down to deeper levels of understanding of this model. Each dimension influences your sales success in an internal, definable way. If gaps occur between these dimensions, your sales ability will weaken. When, through learning and development, these parts begin to converge, your sales ability will increase.

Like perfection, the complete congruence of these elements can never be completely achieved, but any level of growth pays off.

I must emphasize again that this convergence happens over time. Spending a week on each chapter, practicing the Action Guides, and coming back frequently and reviewing the chapters will help you gradually enjoy stronger inner congruence of these elements.

The more you learn about selling, the more you'll learn there is to learn.

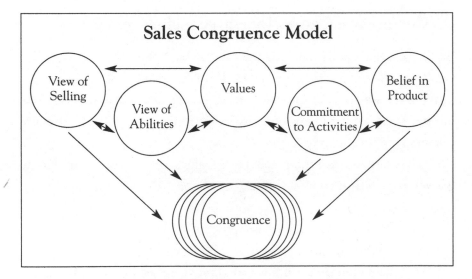

Integrity Selling, or selling with integrity, filters all your actions and behaviors through positive values. Values also provide reference points for you—what's right and what's wrong. They form the boundaries of your beliefs and subsequent behaviors. Some values that influence your selling are:

1. I go the extra mile and give customers more then they expect to get.
2. I do the right thing because it's the right thing to do.
3. I focus on understanding and filling the wants or needs of others, knowing that when I do, my needs will be well filled.
4. I tell the truth in all situations, unless it would hurt someone.
5. I do unto others as I would have them do unto me.
6. I know that I'll enjoy high levels of prosperity if I create high levels of value for *others*.

When these values are demonstrated through your behaviors, a whole new level of energy and confidence is released.

Congruence Causes Increased Achievement Drive

Look back again at the congruence model. After observing tens of thousands of salespeople in our courses, I'm convinced that achievement drive is released only as these dimensions come into a congruence. And as you bring these dimensions into congruence, achievement drive is released proportionately.

Here are the internal beliefs or values that release this latent power from within you:

1. Believing that selling is a process of identifying and filling people's needs.
2. Believing that you have the knowledge, skills, and abilities to sell this way.
3. Believing that the six values listed above are appropriate guides for long-term sales success.
4. Willingness to do the necessary activities to serve customers in the highest manner.

5. Being convinced that your product or service creates value above what your customer pays you.

The strength of these internal beliefs will also determine the amount of the achievement drive you release. The power of your goal achievement will then be consistent with the congruence of these beliefs.

In Integrity Selling language, you choose with your "I Think" to act and respond in certain ways. These actions and responses, when positive and appropriate, then interact with the values in your "I Am" to produce emotions of confidence, enthusiasm, and emotional freedom in your "I Feel." Your emotional intelligence is enhanced and thus influences even stronger actions or responses.

On the other hand, making conscious decisions that conflict with the values in your "I Am" will lead to reduced self-confidence, internal stress, and low activity levels.

Inspiration to Action

As you read this chapter and reflect on the concepts I've presented, ask yourself: "What inspires me to action?"

What causes you to want to blast through your natural comfort plateaus, to push yourself to forge new trails to higher sales goals? What drives you? What would you like to happen in your future that excites you, inspires you, and gives you new levels of energy and confidence? What future rewards are so exciting and compelling that they motivate you to new actions, increased learning, and more successful activity management?

As you identify these external rewards and envision yourself enjoying them, your inner Goal-Seeking Mechanism will silently steer you to them.

This is the secret of self-motivation and to releasing higher levels of achievement drive. Like most other powerful truths, this can also be learned and experienced on many levels.

How to Gain the Most from This Chapter

Here are some simple action steps that will help you cause the powers described in this chapter to go to work for you, helping you move into higher and higher levels of success, self-fulfillment, and service to others:

1. Set sales career, income, or productivity goals.
2. Review the ten motives and select two or three that most fit your own motivational needs.
3. Guided by these motivators, define what you'll give yourself or do for others when you reach your sales or productivity goals.
4. Think daily about the rewards you'll enjoy when your goals are reached, each time visualizing the joy, comfort, recognition, safety, or whatever your desired gratification is.
5. Every time you catch yourself doubting your goal achievement, say, "Stop! Stop thinking negative thoughts!" Then immediately replace these doubts by visualizing the rewards you'll enjoy when you reach your goals.
6. Choose with your "I Think" to practice the six values listed. This will be consistent with values in your "I Am," which in time will cause stronger, more positive emotions to be produced in your "I Feel."

There you have it! A complete process for releasing unlimited achievement drive and achieving an inner congruence. You'll build hope within yourself by feasting your mind on the rewards you'll enjoy when your goals are reached. You'll enjoy new levels of energy and motivation.

You'll discover, as you do this exercise, that it can take you to higher and higher goal achievement.

Its power is unlimited.

[8]

Validate: Cause People to Believe and Trust You

INTEGRITY SELLING SUCCESS PRINCIPLE

**All lasting relationships are built on trust.
People tend to trust us when we're trustworthy people.**

One of my oldest friends and longtime attorney, Warlick Thomas, once described a mutual friend, Bill Johnson, as "having an affidavit face. What he says and does already comes notarized."

Bill Johnson has an unusual combination of gifts. First, under no circumstances would he mislead anyone. He is so nice and conscientious that we've accused him of looking for other people's debts so he can pay them. He's probably the most honest, sincere, yet highly motivated person I've ever known. What makes him a great salesman is that he combines these values with an extremely strong work ethic. Bill has been highly successful because people know they can trust him. After being diagnosed with cancer, he talked bankers into loaning him $9 million. They know that he wouldn't do or say anything unless he believed it was right. *Who* he is validates *what* he does and *how* he's perceived by people.

In Integrity Selling we often must validate ourselves, our products or service, and our organization. When we validate, we successfully answer these basic questions that are in customers' minds:

1. Can I believe and trust you?
2. Can I have confidence in the value of your product or service?
3. Can I be assured that your organization will stand behind this sale?

Sometimes, because of strong brand recognition, people buy things from people they don't particularly like. Other times, people purchase new brands despite the poor skills of the salesperson, because they're loyal to the larger organization. Still other times, people buy because they like and trust the salesperson.

The more that a purchaser can say "yes" to all three of the above questions, the stronger the chances of a sale. All healthy, long-lasting customer relationships are based on trust, integrity, and mutual respect.

An Ongoing Process

Let me emphasize that validation isn't a separate step in the AID,Inc. system, although the graph shows it as such. Really, it's a process that begins with first impressions and goes on throughout the buyer/seller relationship.

The reason we place it where we do in the AID,Inc. system is that until we have validated, or caused potential purchasers to trust us and believe our claims, we weaken our chances to negotiate and close. Any time trust and confidence are missing, our chances for a sale are weakened.

The validation process begins with first impressions. People's initial feelings are formed in several subtle ways—through brand advertising, word of mouth, physical appearance of the business or salespeople, and initial treatment.

These feelings and relationships are further developed as time goes on.

Validation Action Guides

These four Action Guides will help you validate your product or service:

1. Translate product or service features into customer benefits.
2. Justify price and emphasize value.
3. Offer proof and evidence.
4. Reassure and reinforce people to neutralize their fear of buying.

Think for a few moments about how you can apply each of these in your selling.

Translate Product or Service Features into Customer Benefits

As I explained in Chapter 6, most people don't buy product or service features. They buy end-result benefits. Features are what make up the product or service; benefits are what customers will enjoy as a result of having them. It's important to understand the difference.

While this seems quite logical, as you observe ten salespeople at work, you'll find that most are product-focused rather than customer benefits-focused. They tend to spend most of their time talking about what their product or service is, rather than the benefits customers will enjoy as a result of having it.

Successful salespeople know not to overly dwell on features, but to explain only the ones that will give customers the benefits they individually want.

As you've learned, it's during the Interview step that you find out people's wants or needs. It's also when you begin to determine your customers' dominant buying motives, or their main reasons for buying.

Dominant Buying Motives

The main dominant buying motives are *pride*, *profit*, *pleasure*, and *peace*.

1. *Pride*—to feel a sense of accomplishment; to look good to others; to feel respected or admired by others; to know that others know that you have what you have.
2. *Profit*—to increase; to gain; to enjoy measurable rewards; to get a good deal.
3. *Pleasure*—to gratify a desire; to enjoy a better lifestyle; to go places and do fun things; to please the senses.
4. *Peace*—to enjoy peace of mind and security; to insure against potential loss; to remove possible obstacles; to reduce risks.

These basic buying motives drive people's purchase decisions. It's important to know what dominant buying motives drive your customers' decisions, so you can serve them better. You'll often discover, later in a sales process, that you didn't uncover your customer's real motives. When you're not sure about their motives, you should go back for more fact-finding and attempt to understand them. For example, dig deeper and find out:

1. Why do they want what you're selling?
2. What rewards, benefits, or gratification do they want your product or service to give them?
3. What is their level of desire for these end-result benefits or rewards?
4. Whom do they want to please with this purchase?

5. What is their level of urgency to make a purchase?
6. What is their behavior style?

Once you understand people's dominant buying motives, along with their sense of urgency, you can then explain how your product or service features will give them the benefits they desire. Keep your focus on their reasons for buying, not your reasons for selling. Fit your solutions into their dominant buying motives.

Admittedly, you may have only limited time with your customers and won't be able to understand these deep drives. But the more you want to understand their motives, the more you'll intuitively learn more about them.

Justify Price and Emphasize Value

Before anyone makes a purchase decision, they either consciously or unconsciously answer this question: "Do the benefits I'll enjoy from this purchase exceed the cost that I'll pay for it?"

They say "no" because, in their minds, the cost exceeds the perceived benefits. They say "yes" because they believe that the value or benefits exceeds the cost.

Because the actual monetary cost is often thought to be a buyer's main consideration, I'll stop a moment and emphasize that *cost* can be several things. It could include:

1. Money
2. Time
3. Risk
4. Potential problems
5. Potential mistake of purchase
6. Negative responses of other people

These are only a few of the concerns that make up "cost." It's necessary for you to understand what your customers consider their "cost" before you can make the cost/benefit comparison. The more you understand their specific cost concerns, the more you'll know what to validate. In fact, until you know this, your validation will probably be hit-or-miss.

I'll explain more about how you can remove concerns from customers' minds in Chapter 10.

Offer Proof and Evidence

How do you prove your product or service claims? When you explain the value or end-result benefits you can give people, and they say "prove it," how do you do it? What evidence do you have that backs up your claims?

Obviously, the more expensive, high tech, complicated, or intangible your product or service is, the more proof your customers will probably want that they'll enjoy the benefits you promised. Organizations spend lots of money on research, studies, or reports to back up their claims and give their customers a sense of security.

Clinical tests for drugs, crash tests for vehicles, the Good Housekeeping Seal of Approval for a laundry detergent, and the American Dental Association approval for a toothpaste are all examples of ways in which organizations validate their products or services. Testimonial letters, personal endorsements from famous people, or reports from satisfied users can also help validate your claims.

A word of warning: You can often offer too much proof or evidence, and flood customers with a lot more information than they want to know. Keep your proof tailored only to your customer's specific concerns.

Reassure and Reinforce People to
Neutralize Their Fear of Buying

Depending on their behavior style, many people are risk aversive, resistant to change, or reluctant to make decisions. These behaviors may have less to do with their perception of the value/cost equation than with their individual apprehension about making decisions, along with their natural behavior style. When you're able to recognize different people's emotions as they face decisions, you will know exactly how to proceed with them.

Here are some basic ideas about the natural tendencies that different behavior styles exhibit as they begin to reach a decision or move through a purchase process:

- Doers love to make decisions. They'll often make them based on their trust of you. They'll be influenced by other high-profile people who have bought from you. Mainly, they'll be motivated by their perceived bottom-line benefits to themselves. Let the decision be their own idea. Let them tell you what their benefits will be. Remember that they'll be motivated by benefits that help them achieve results or help them appear in charge.

- Talkers don't enjoy making decisions. They're concerned about what others will think of them. They may even want to please and impress you. They need reassurance that other people will approve of their purchase decisions. They want to bring enjoyment and pleasure to their peers, friends, or family. They often need help in making decisions. Their indecision may be caused by their reluctance to reject you. They find it very difficult to say "no" to anyone.

- Controllers need facts and logical proof. They'll question the accuracy of your claims, and will cut you off if your proof isn't accurate and well documented. They won't be swayed by your enthusiasm or friendliness. They'll make very rational decisions once they see evidence and proof that what you're selling will eliminate risks and get the results you claim. They're driven by logic, not emotions.

- Supporters often avoid risk since their main motivation is to seek security and please other people. They'll make slow decisions, and will want validation that's well established and conservative. They're less motivated by rewards or end-result benefits than by the reduction of risk. Clearly understand their perceptions of risks, attempt to remove them, give them time, and help them see a safe course.

The Three Fear Points of Buyers

Fear can keep people from making purchase decisions even when they want what you're selling. The thought of making a commitment to buy something can make many people anxious. But you can help people move through their fear when you understand at what points it happens. Generally, people have three basic fear points:

1. When you approach them, they ask themselves, "Can I handle this person in this situation?"
2. Just before making a buying decision, they ask themselves, "What if I do this and later regret it?"
3. Just after making a purchase commitment, they ask themselves, "Have I done the right thing?"

As you move through the purchasing process with your customers, notice their reactions—their eye contact, body language, voice level, and how close they want you to stand or sit. Watch for other telltale signs of concern, fear, apprehension, openness, excitement, or other positive or negative reactions. Carefully listen to their comments. Are they looking for reasons to buy, or focusing too much on risks?

Your observation can clue you in to people's concerns and allow you to give appropriate understanding, support, or reassurance to them.

Offer Benefits Consistent with
Your Customer's Self-Image

A number of years ago, Prescott Lecky, an educator, coined a concept that he called the *Theory of Self-Consistency* in a book titled *Self-Consistency: A Theory of Personality*. He conceived that our individual personalities are a system of ideas, beliefs, and values that are made up of, or seem consistent with, our actions, decisions, and behaviors.

Lecky went on to say that people accept ideas that seem consistent with the ideas, beliefs, and values they've *already accepted*. They also tend to reject new ideas that seem *to conflict* with their old, established ones.

Although he was an educator, not a salesperson, Lecky's ideas offer those of us who sell some very important validation points. For instance, *your customers will experience a powerful inner motivation to accept your solutions or benefits when they're presented in a way that's consistent with who they perceive themselves to be.*

Please stop and read this again. Relate it to some of your actual customer experiences. Don't rush past it and leave it as merely an intellectual concept.

I've violated this principle many times, only to discover that I failed to understand *who* or *what* my customers' self-perceptions were, or the benefits that would have helped them carry out their individual self-perceptions.

An old friend who had been very successful in business told me a story about going to a dentist's office. After a thorough examination, the doctor recommended a rather expensive treatment plan. My friend's immediate response was "That's more than I can afford." He asked, "Isn't there a less expensive method of treatment?"

"Yes, of course there is," the doctor replied, "but this is the one I'd recommend for someone who's been as successful as you!"

My friend laughed and said, "It then took me about thirteen seconds to reconsider and say 'yes' to his full treatment plan."

People will usually act and respond consistently with who they perceive themselves to be.

Understand People's Unique Self-Perceptions

Dr. Lecky believed that virtually everyone possesses what he called an *ego-ideal*, or a picture of who we want to be. He found that most of us have an inner need to think of ourselves as self-reliant, capable of standing on our own two feet. We want to be perceived as able to do our part. We want to be respected, and to contribute something worthwhile to others. We all have our own definition of how we want others to view us and we want our opinions and behavior to be looked upon favorably.

You'll sell more when you present product or service benefits consistent with your customer's views of who they are. Rather than doing this, though, many salespeople hold fast to their own *ego-ideals* and allow them to clash with their customers' self-perceptions. Salespeople's attitudes of "I'm an expert, and I know what's best for you" can draw battle lines between them and their customers, a battle that salespeople can never win.

When you present ideas and benefits to customers and show that you expect them to be fair in their evaluation, you appeal to their *ego-ideal*. Studies show that when you view customers as being fair, honest, and conscientious in their dealings with you, this reinforcement alone carries powerful validation. While some people don't respond in a fair, honest way, they're a minority.

If you treat people fairly, they'll usually treat you fairly.

See Yourself As a Value Creator

Perceived value is the greatest motivator of customers. Every purchase is made because of some intrinsic value that the buyer perceives he or she will enjoy. This value might be tangible, psychological, social, or may fill other unique needs a person wants satisfied.

Rarely is price alone the main determinant of value; rather, it's included in a mix of several factors. Customers have different perceptions of what value is to them. Notice the following model as a thought process that customers go through before making a decision.

The Perceived Value Process from the Customer's Viewpoint

- *How I'll look*
- *How I'll feel*
- *What I'll enjoy*
- *How I'll be protected*
- *How others will think of me* $\div$ *Price = Perceived Value*
- *How long it'll last*
- *How proud I'll be of it*
- *How much I need it*
- *How badly I want it*

In order to generate value and present an offering that's consistent with your customers' perceived needs and views of who they are, you first must know what your customers perceive value to be. It helps to first get an idea of who they perceive themselves to be. While you probably can't know everything about customers' total needs—maybe your sale has a short closing cycle—knowing just a little will help. Looking and listening increases your awareness, and helps you discover a customer's motivations when you might not otherwise think about them.

Keep in mind that the Validation step isn't necessarily a separate step of AID,Inc.; it's an ongoing process. Numerous factors influence customers' trust and belief in us throughout the sale. I'll pull these factors together in this chapter, explaining how they occur at different AID,Inc. steps.

A Healthy View of Selling Unconsciously Validates Us to Our Customers

Salespeople with the healthiest and highest self-esteem don't have overblown egos. These highly successful salespeople view their job as creating value for customers. This is a very healthy view of selling. Serving. Helping. Focusing on solutions. Salespeople who focus on *making sales* will never enjoy the long-term success, client respect, or self-esteem of those who focus on creating more and better value for customers.

When our business associates first begin to talk to organizations about their current sales and service culture, we find that most misunderstand customer-focused selling. Many think that *selling* is a dirty word.

I remember one of our associates approaching members of a large, national company, highly respected for their integrity and service, who told him, "We don't sell, we serve!"

"Let's make sure we understand you," our associate replied. "Describe what you mean when you use the word 'service.'"

"It's understanding the needs of our customers and then helping them fill them," they replied.

"That's how we define Integrity Selling," he responded. He then went on to emphasize that our definitions of *selling* and *service* are really the same. Both are processes of identifying wants, needs, problems, challenges, risks, or goals people have. Both involve helping internal or external customers reach, satisfy, or enjoy their needs or objectives.

After more discussion, the client allowed us to demonstrate our Integrity Selling process for their evaluation. It worked far beyond their expectations, and we now enjoy a wonderful client relationship; we aim to help them enjoy rewards far greater than what they pay us.

View of Selling Influences Your Strength and Energy

Do you remember the kinesiology experiment I told you about in Chapter 7 that demonstrated how your strength increases when you focus on the rewards of higher selling? We also use it in our training sessions to demonstrate the power of a positive view of selling. We ask people to stand, hold their arms out parallel to the floor, then we test their arm strength by gradually pulling down on them. We then ask them to silently say to themselves several times, "I believe that selling is doing or saying anything I have to do or say just to get people to buy from me."

After six to eight seconds, we test their arm strength again, only to discover that they've lost up to 90 percent of their strength.

Then we ask them to take a deep breath and relax for a moment. After a few seconds, we ask them to say to themselves, "I believe that selling is identifying and filling people's needs, and creating value for them." We test their arm strength again, only to discover that all their original strength, plus some, has returned.

This isn't smoke and mirrors. It's very real. You can do it with *your* salespeople. When you focus on identifying and filling people's needs, with the objective of creating value above the cost of what you're paid, you'll have higher energy and confidence, and a stronger sense of purpose.

Your Values and Attitudes Are Projected to Customers

I believe that more interpersonal communication takes place on the subliminal "I Am" level than on the conscious "I Think" one.

Often without logically processing it, people form pretty quick impressions of us. While these opinions exist on a subliminal level, they powerfully motivate customers' responses to us. Do they feel good about us? Do they view us as being professional? Do they think they can trust us? These and many other thoughts run through their minds.

We communicate in these ways:

1.   Observable, logical: "What I see in you."
2.   Feelings, emotional: "How I feel about you."
3.   Intuitive, sixth sense: "What I sense about you."

I believe that people unconsciously make intuitive assumptions about us. "The wisdom of the unconscious," as Dr. Carl Jung wrote, is the ability discern the values, intentions, and attitudes of others.

I believe people with strong, positive beliefs communicate them to others through powerful, unconscious avenues without even trying. Something deep within my customers tells them they can trust me.

Because I believe in integrity, honesty, and sincerity, and have the genuine desire to create value for others, this becomes my strongest form of validation. "Who you are speaks so loudly that I can't hear what you say" was written by Emerson many years ago. It's still true today.

People ask me often, "How do I get people to trust me?" My response is "By being a person that people *can* trust." Trust results from who you are in your "I Am," not what you say from your "I Think."

Being a person that customers can trust is a sure way to validate yourself. When people see values-driven behaviors in you, they intuitively, through their *sixth sense*, feel your sincerity; you can achieve a very high form of validation.

Remember, all lasting relationships are built upon mutual trust.

How to Know When You've Completed the Validation Step

1.   People seem to trust you and believe your claims.
2.   They are convinced of the efficacy of your product or service.

3. They believe that your organization will stand behind your product or service performance.
4. They respect you for your integrity.

How to Gain the Most from This Chapter

Write these Action Guides on an index card and carry them next week:

1. Translate product or service features into customer benefits.
2. Justify price and emphasize value.
3. Offer proof and evidence.
4. Reassure and reinforce people to neutralize their fear of buying.

Refer to your card several times each day and practice the guides at every opportunity.

Reflect often on your view of selling. How do you reveal your beliefs in your own thinking and selling activities? Do you focus on making a sale or on satisfying your customers' admitted wants or needs?

Go back and review the kinesiology demonstrations that I described. Get with a friend or a neutral third party and practice them. See what happens. It will probably blow your mind.

Spend some time thinking of people you know who live by strong, positive internal values. Observe them. Notice their confidence and energy level. Notice how other people trust and have confidence in them.

Make sure that you're selling something in which you believe— that you're convinced you'll bring more value to your clients or customers than they'll pay for. Be able to say to your customers after the sale has been consummated, "You can count on me to give you much more than I'm being paid."

This *extra mile* philosophy will guarantee your long-term success. You'll begin to carry yourself and communicate like a person of substance. Your customers will know you're a professional.

Integrity means doing the right thing because it's the right thing to do.

[9]

Winning Over
Negative Emotions

One of my good friends and mentors Jerry Little and I talked for many years about our mutual love of selling. After spending over thirty years as an agency manager for American General Life, he was a real pro. One day, during lunch, he said, "Most young life insurance agents learn quickly how to deal with call reluctance!"

"They do?" I eagerly asked, thinking that I was about to hear one of the great secrets of the ages. "How?"

"Yeah, they quit making calls," he replied.

Like many thoughts of wise people, Jerry's point was quick and right on target. Scores of books have been written about why salespeople fail or settle for low levels of sales, but none could sum it up more succinctly than Jerry's statement.

Salespeople's inability to deal with fear of rejection, fear of failure, fear of the unknown, and even fear of success will probably cause them to fail more than anything else.

But is there a cure to this common malady? Yes. I'll share it with you in this chapter.

But first, I must warn you. Often the way people fight their fears is self-defeating. If you only use discipline or willpower to push out negative, destructive thoughts, you're not only setting yourself up to fail, you're probably worsening the very problem you're trying to solve.

The secret is not to push negative, fearful thoughts out of your mind, but to *replace* them with positive ones. I'll call this process *thought substitution*, and here's how it works. Whenever you catch yourself thinking negative, fearful thoughts, immediately say to yourself, "Stop!" Then replace them with positive thoughts. For example, as the time draws near to ask for a purchase decision, you may suddenly emotionally freeze up, afraid that the answer will be "no" rather than "yes." When this happens, say to yourself, "Stop! Stop expecting a negative response, and remember the value you will create for your customer!"

Then immediately visualize the benefits your customer will enjoy from the transaction.

Perhaps you need to telephone for an appointment, but every time you begin to dial the number, your hand shakes and you think, "I probably can't get past this person's assistant." Suddenly the fear of the unknown sets in. As you recognize this, cradle your telephone for a minute and say, "Stop. Stop expecting negative responses."

Then replace these negative thoughts with a statement like "I believe I can help this person [or organization], and I have a professional responsibility to them to find out if they have needs I can help fill!"

Your thoughts trigger certain emotions, and these lead to specific actions. Do this *thought substitution* consistently, and within a few weeks you'll do it automatically.

In time, this process will help you create more successful actions.

The Main Challenge of Selling Success

Our inner emotional controls can either shut off or open the floodgates to high achievement in selling. Few people are bombarded with more negative responses than salespeople. The average salesperson probably hears *no* much more than any other word. Absorbing that kind of rejection can take its toll, unless you know how to maintain your emotional control. For many, this is the main challenge in selling.

Over the years, I've conditioned myself to deal with the ups and downs of selling in a fairly level way. I used to get emotionally high when I made a sale, only to experience an emotional low when I didn't make one. Unconsciously, I equated either making or not making a sale as an acceptance or rejection of me as a person. I had to overcome that limiting belief before I could move forward. I had to learn that when people said "no" to me, it meant they were rejecting my ideas, not me.

Once I understood my problem, I devised a self-suggestion that helped strengthen deep beliefs in my "I Am." The self-suggestion was: *People aren't rejecting me; they're rejecting my offer!*

As I repeated this over time, this thought became lodged deeply within my beliefs. I began to separate my personal feelings of worth from people saying "no" to my product or service. I accepted the fact that not everyone had a perceived need for what I sold.

Separating self-worth from outside influences is essential for long-term sales success.

Let's face it, we're human. Fear and negative emotions are a fact of life. The few salespeople that I've known who didn't experience them faced other difficulties. Usually the emotions that prevented them from experiencing fear also dulled their ability to listen, understand, and care for others. Salespeople who are out of touch with their own feelings are also often out of touch with their customers' sensitivities.

Often salespeople who don't have call reluctance, or fear of rejection, are unable to pick up on their customers' responses. By failing to listen and understand, they are less able to meet their customers' needs.

Rather than trying to get rid of negative emotions, you should transform them into positive energies by *thought substitution*. I'll explain other ways of thought replacement in this chapter.

Selling Is a Holistic Issue

Since selling is mainly an emotional issue, you must ask: How can I understand the feelings I experience, and determine whether I should keep, replace, or control them?

Your "I Think," "I Feel," and "I Am" work in a holistic manner— each dimension interacting to produce different outcomes. You'll notice this is my central message of this book, which I present on many different levels. From time to time, I've reminded you of some fundamental truths, with the hope that you'll understand them on deeper levels over time.

With this in mind, here are several ways to understand and control your emotions.

Understanding Your Emotions

The Three Dimensions of Human Behavior model that I presented earlier will help you understand a bit more about what triggers your emotions. More important, though, it will give you a guide for converting your negative feelings into positive, constructive, success-driving ones.

Please review the following model and read the functions of each of the three dimensions.

Study the chart on the next page for a few moments. Now read the following keys to understanding it:

1. Choices made in your "I Think" interact with the programming in your "I Am" and trigger either positive or negative emotions in your "I Feel."

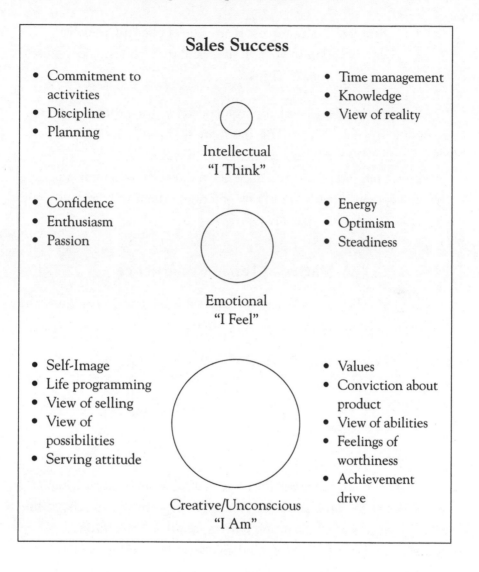

Sales Success

- Commitment to
  activities
- Discipline
- Planning

Intellectual
"I Think"

- Time management
- Knowledge
- View of reality

- Confidence
- Enthusiasm
- Passion

Emotional
"I Feel"

- Energy
- Optimism
- Steadiness

- Self-Image
- Life programming
- View of selling
- View of
  possibilities
- Serving attitude

Creative/Unconscious
"I Am"

- Values
- Conviction about
  product
- View of abilities
- Feelings of
  worthiness
- Achievement
  drive

2. Knowing what to do in your "I Think" without doing it
   interacts with values in your "I Am" and produces negative
   emotions of low self-confidence in your "I Feel."
3. Weak programming in your "I Am," such as a negative view
   of selling, will negate knowledge in your "I Think" and cause
   destructive emotions in your "I Feel."

4. Ultimately, sales success is an issue of planting positive, healthy beliefs in your "I Am," and then choosing congruent actions in your "I Think."

Success in selling is mainly influenced by strengthening the programming in your "I Am." This has more to do with an inner congruence than with a forced discipline or use of willpower.

I must remind you, again, to go beyond reading and understanding the concepts in this book; only by practicing them in your real-world experiences will you gradually reprogram your "I Am."

A Matter of Inner Congruence

In Chapter 3, I shared a Sales Congruence Model and gave you some action steps to strengthen each of the five dimensions:

1. View of selling
2. View of abilities
3. Values
4. Commitment to activities
5. Belief in product

From time to time, you'll find it helpful to go back to Chapter 3 and select some of the action steps and practice them. Integrity selling should be a continuing learning process, not a one-time thing.

For the rest of this chapter, I'll go deeper into actions you can take to strengthen your "I Am"—which is how you build successful habits and behaviors.

Let's start at the beginning of your day.

Make a No-Withdrawal Commitment

Salespeople begin each day with one of the two levels of job commitment. Consciously or unconsciously, they either say:

- *If this job works out, I'll stay in it!*
- *I'll stay in this job and make it work out.*

Two different attitudes. Two different levels of commitment. And ultimately, two vastly different ultimate levels of success.

I've worked with many different kinds of sales organizations, some with very low levels of turnover, others with much higher rates. I've tried to understand what determines this gap, and I've concluded that the difference in the people who succeed from those who drop out is the commitment they make to it.

Have you made a no-withdrawal commitment to your current sales job? Are you with a company that you feel good about, where you have high potential to excel? Are you selling products or services that you believe in and want people to have? Do you view your role of selling as identifying and filling customers' needs and creating value that exceeds your payment? Do your organization's values and sales ethics match yours?

If you can answer *yes* to these questions, then you're probably in the right place, selling the right product or service. Now you must make a strong commitment to stay with it and grow.

You may want to take some time this week and write down the positive things your current job offers you. Then write down the negative factors that could cause you to quit or give a halfhearted effort to your job. These could be anything from slow markets to a lack of personal confidence. Make your list as long as you can, and be honest.

Look at your list. What you wrote down are probably the same roadblocks that both weak and successful salespeople have faced for ages. The difference is that successful salespeople work through them.

After reviewing your list, ask yourself this question: "Am I willing to work through these difficulties in order to be successful in what I'm doing?"

Almost all highly successful salespeople have asked themselves this question, and they've answered it by responding, "Yes, I'm willing to face and work through these roadblocks. I accept that this is the initiation fee that I must pay to enter the club of high achievers. And, although I don't want to have to deal with these issues, I will because I want to be highly successful!"

Asking and answering this question over and over will help you build your persistence and determination.

Once you know deep within your "I Am" that you'll work through any difficulty that attempts to stop you, you'll reach a new level of confidence, sense of destiny, and success consciousness.

Actions Change Feelings

People who give in to their negative feelings often fail because they misinterpret the truth about themselves. The truth is that your negative feelings don't determine who you are; your actions reveal who you are. Few people escape having negative thoughts or feelings. But people who transcend the control or grip of negative emotions have learned the difference. When encountering negative circumstances or emotions, they say: "*You* will not determine my success. I will determine it!"

Learn to treat negative feelings or circumstances as personal enemies. Challenge them. Face them. Grit your teeth. Clench your fist. Slug it out with them. Talk to them—tell them that you're stronger than they are. Let them know that they can't win. Let your full competitive nature come out.

After challenging negative influences, take some kind of immediate positive action. Don't brood, stew, analyze, or fret. Do something. Do what you're afraid to do, go where you're afraid to go, ask when you're afraid to ask. Any small step in a positive direction will tend to neutralize fear or negative emotions. Here's an important self-management principle: Action overcomes fear. Your fears aren't under the direct control of your conscious thoughts, logic, or knowledge—but they are under the direct control of your actions.

Action, or doing the thing you fear, always reduces anxiety or other negative feelings. As the wise William James wrote, "Do the thing you fear, and the death of fear is certain."

Anytime you find your self-confidence shaken, or your anxiety level rising, make a conscious decision in your "I Think" to take some positive action. Then immediately do it. You'll automatically strengthen your "I Am," which will begin to produce more positive emotions and replace the negative ones.

Choosing to do the thing you fear always enhances your unconscious view of yourself, causing you to experience more positive emotions and helping you strengthen your ability to make further choices and decisions. This explains the cycle of growth. You hold the key to facing your negative emotions through the actions you choose to take.

This is a proactive strategy to take, but there are other powerful yet indirect ways to build your confidence and repel fear.

Your View of Selling

I've mentioned it before, but let's think more about your view of selling for a moment. It begins with an intellectual understanding in your "I Think" that selling is a process of filling needs and creating value for people that exceed what they pay you.

I've discovered that when salespeople view the sales process as getting people to do something *for* them, this view weakens them. But when they view selling as a process of *doing something for people*, a transforming power takes place within them. Confidence increases. Fear of rejection decreases. Self-esteem rises.

Trying to get people to make a decision solely for your benefit breeds a *first-person sensitivity*. People with this attitude are overly focused on their own needs and how they're perceived. On the other hand, salespeople with a *second-person sensitivity* are focused on what customers' needs are, and how to communicate and understand them. One view is: *Please understand me and my product or service.* The other one is: *Please help me understand you and your unique wants or needs.*

Again, we see this paradox—the more salespeople focus on them-selves and their needs, the weaker their sales results will be. But the more they focus on their customers' needs, the stronger they become and the more sales they'll close.

Your View of Your Abilities

Once you begin saturating your "I Am" with a positive view of selling and applying the AID,Inc. system, you'll notice an amazing surge in your energy, confidence, and enthusiasm.

But those salespeople who view selling as doing something *to* cus-tomers are often dissatisfied with their jobs and don't know why.

Values

Values are the rules by which you live your life. They govern your actions and behavior. They are at the deepest foundation of your "I Am." Your values help you distinguish between right and wrong. As you go through life, you're constantly consciously or unconsciously defining your values. When faced with problems or difficulties, you'll need to answer the following questions with your actions. As you do, your values are automatically demonstrated.

- *How will I handle this problem?*
- *Will I tell the truth when a half-truth might get me over the hump?*
- *Will I present my product or service claims correctly?*
- *Will I make the calls, contacts, or follow-up activities that I commit to doing?*
- *Will I focus on how much I can get or how much I can give?*
- *Will I take shortcuts or will I build solid foundations for long-term success?*
- *Will I take responsibility for my actions, or will I blame others?*

- *Will I be open to learn from others—even those who criticize me?*
- *Will I look for my life's purpose?*
- *Will I view problems and personal weaknesses as learning aids?*

What Are Your Values?

What inviolable ethics, or life principles, guide your decisions, choices, behaviors, or actions? Have you clearly defined them? Do you treat them with such respect that they become your most valuable attributes? Few factors will influence your long-term sales success as much as these healthy rules of conduct. They'll help increase your purpose, confidence, self-esteem, and physical as well as emotional energy. They'll cause you to have a stronger bearing as you interact with people.

Additionally, when you're selling, your strong, healthy, positive values are subliminally communicated from your "I Am" to your customers' "I Am." My years of training and development have shown me the power of salespeople's strong values upon customer relationships.

Positive values are one of the most powerful forces behind successful selling.

Commitment to Activities

Many sales managers manage their people by measuring activities: keeping track of the number of contacts you make to set up appointments, how many actual sales calls you make, business lunches you attend, etc. While all these are necessary for certain types of sales, the principle is weak.

Most salespeople whose activities are measured will reach only low to moderate levels of sales success. Since activities can be faked or misreported, 80 percent of salespeople who are managed this way will unconsciously do the required activities and then shut down. They'll almost never reach high sales results. We see this all the time.

"But activities are necessary," you're probably saying. And, of course, you're correct. But activities are only significant if they help us reach sales goals. When activities are your goals, low sales usually result because often the selected activities are only tension-relieving ones, not result-producing ones.

I learned many years ago that salespeople will choose result-producing activities only when:

1. They have goal clarity.
2. They have sufficient levels of achievement drive, and
3. Their view of selling, view of their abilities, and values are all congruent.

Only when we view selling as a process of helping people, when we believe we can be successful doing it, and when what we're asked to do aligns with our values are we able to do the right activities. And not only will we want to do the necessary activities, we'll feel an obligation to do them in order to help as many people as possible.

To take this a step further: When you view selling as creating value for people, and believe that you'll be rewarded to the degree that you help people, you'll also believe that you should be highly rewarded.

This belief is called "prosperity consciousness," and we'll explain it further in Chapter 11.

Belief in Product

I pity the people who sell a product or service because they feel they must. I admire people who sell things because they honestly believe their product or service will create more value for their customers than what they receive in return.

It's the surplus, the extra value that exceeds what people pay for products or services, that drives sales success and creates lasting relationships. Look at it like this:

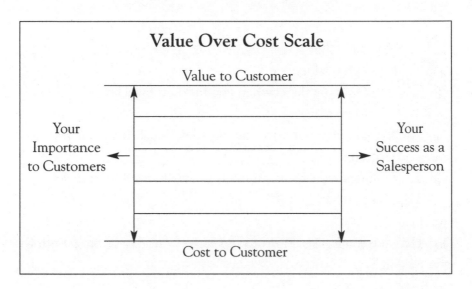

Value Over Cost Scale

To what extent do you believe the value you give customers exceeds the cost they pay you? What affects it? What can you do to continually increase it?

Remember . . . the size of the gap between the actual value you bring to your customers and the price it costs them will determine the level of long-term success you enjoy. When this inner value is in your "I Am," and is demonstrated by your behavior, it triggers immense levels of passion, conviction, and confidence in your "I Feel." You'll act and perform on a much higher level than most other salespeople, and customers will notice.

How to Gain the Most from This Chapter

Here are some basic activities that will help you strengthen the programming in your "I Am," which will then produce positive emotions in your "I Feel," which will come back around to strengthen future choices and actions you make in your "I Think."

1. Write on a card each evening:
   a. A customer or client's name.

    b.   A need they may have that you can help them fill.

    c.   How they'll feel when you fill their need and give them extra value.

    d.   How you'll feel when you fill their need and give them extra value.

2.   Spend ten minutes in a quiet place, visualizing what you've written down.

3.   Command your subconscious to dwell on this during your night's sleep.

Here are some suggestions to repeat to yourself and program into your "I Am":

1.   I believe that selling is identifying and filling people's needs, and creating value for them.

2.   I have the ability to sell this way.

3.   I owe it to my customers to create as much value for them as I can.

4.   I know that I'll be compensated in self-respect, customer respect, self-confidence, and money (if appropriate) consistent with the value I create for customers.

Spend a week on this chapter. Read it over several times. Underline or highlight certain points. Make notes in the margin of these pages. Pick out one or two highly successful and respected salespeople and study their behaviors, values, and attitudes. Learn from them. Plan out each day and commit to result-producing activities and then do them.

Be driven by purpose. You owe it to your customers to create as much value for them as you can. When you catch yourself using willpower or discipline to drive your activities, stop and refocus on your responsibility of creating value for them. Keep visualizing the value you give over the cost. Try each day to increase the gap between cost to them and the value they'll enjoy. Amazing things will happen to your confidence, energy, self-respect, and customer loyalty.

Remember, success in selling is often paradoxical. The more you focus on your need to make a sale, the less you'll enjoy real success. The more you focus on your customers' needs and your need to create value for them, the more you'll sell.

I realize that this contradicts our natural, human, ego-focused drives. But it does work.

Try it, and you'll see for yourself.

[10]

Negotiate: Work Out Problems That Keep People from Buying

INTEGRITY SELLING SUCCESS PRINCIPLE

People are more apt to listen and to understand your point of view when you listen to and understand theirs.

When you hear the word *negotiation,* what immediately comes to mind? If we asked people on the street what they think of when they hear this word, would their responses be mostly positive or negative?

Let's face it, the word conjures up images of offers and counteroffers, haggling, or mental chess games to see who backs down first.

Our definition of negotiation usually reveals our actual view of selling. Is it win-lose, lose-win, or win-win? Is it an issue of whether either you or your customer must win, or one where you both win?

Integrity Negotiation Defined

The Integrity Selling definition of negotiation is: A process of working out the problems or concerns that keep people from buying—when they want to work them out.

There's a major difference between our definition and that of many others. Often, negotiation has been defined as a process of convincing people to change their position and see things your way. This view pits the salesperson against the customer in a game of wits or endurance.

Unfortunately, many businesses still operate this way. Try to buy a car, and see what kind of "negotiation" techniques some dealerships use.

Fortunately, major cultural and value shifts in the last couple of decades have caused many businesses to abandon this old, combative type of customer/salesperson pitted negotiation. Still, many organizations have a long way to go to be truly customer-focused.

The Wreckage Left After Combative Negotiation

Our Integrity Systems business associates have implemented our Integrity Selling curriculum in over two thousand different organizations. We've worked with organizations that sell tangible products and ones that sell intangible services. We've helped companies with as few as ten salespeople and ones with thousands. In our largest sale we trained twenty-six thousand salespeople and managers from nine hundred dealerships at Chevrolet in just the first year.

We've worked with many different cultures with different values and ethics. Some organizations, because of their own strong values and ethics, were ready for our programs. Others weren't. We've noticed when organizations view selling as a process of profiting at customers' expense, have seen the grim results of high salesperson turnover and stress, low customer satisfaction and loyalty, low employee morale, and a host of other side effects of this stress.

Focus on the Front End,
Not the Back End

We've discovered a powerful principle of negotiation. When salespeople focus on gaining rapport with and understanding of their customers' needs—and demonstrating a solution that their customers agree will fill their needs—the need for negotiation decreases and takes on a different form. The principle is this: When trust and rapport are strong, negotiation becomes a partnership to work through customer concerns. But when trust and rapport are weak, almost any negotiation becomes too combative.

When we worked with Chevrolet, we told them that if salespeople would focus on the Approach and Interview steps, rather than on their typical negotiation or price haggling, they'd sell more at better gross profits. We believe that when salespeople take time to truly understand customers' needs, and conscientiously try to recommend the best vehicle to fill those needs, their sales will go up. And they do. Often dramatically.

In an initial pilot with twelve dealers, we improved dealers' closing ratios from one in five to one in four. But that's not all. By doing AID,Inc., their gross profits on sales increased 31 percent, a huge jump. Their success proved our belief that when trust and rapport are developed and relationships are established, price becomes less of a factor.

Let's move on to the Negotiation Action Guides:

1.   Find out what concerns or objections remain.
2.   Welcome and understand objections.
3.   Identify and isolate specific objections.
4.   Discuss possible solutions—ask their opinions for best solutions.

Find Out What Concerns or Objections Remain

Let's set the stage. You've only entered the negotiation stage when customers have:

1. Admitted a need and a desire for a solution, and agreed to talk to you about a solution.
2. Liked your solution, and agreed that it will fill their needs.
3. Expressed concerns, questions, or problems that still need to be worked out.
4. Agreed that they want to work through their concerns or objectives.

Until these steps have been completed, any attempted negotiation is premature.

To answer your customer's questions or challenges, you'll first want to find out what concerns or objections they have. The way to know is to ask questions like these:

- *What other questions do you have?*
- *What other information do you need?*
- *What concern, if any, do you have?*
- *Whom else should we talk to before making a decision?*
- *What other things do you need to consider before making a decision?*
- *As you review our discussions, will my solution fill your needs to your satisfaction?*
- *What else do we need to discuss?*

These and similar questions, altered to fit your customers' specific situations, not only can help you understand their position but can also help them clarify their thinking. The answers to these questions often reveal that you didn't finish your interview or demonstration. You may discover that they didn't:

1. Admit a need or want, admit a desire for a solution, and agree to talk to you about them.
2. Believe your solution will fill or satisfy their wants or needs.
3. Have a sense of urgency to make a decision.

Have the Courage to Face the Truth

Asking for opinions or responses works only when you really want to know what people are thinking. I've often caught myself wanting to slide past my clients' objections—thinking, I suppose, that ignoring them would make them go away.

I learned one of the most helpful self-suggestions from W. Clement Stone: "Have the courage to face the truth!" I've repeated that affirmation to myself many times.

Repeating that self-suggestion over time programmed it into my mind. When the programming was done, every time I found myself in a situation where I was reluctant to ask questions because I was afraid of getting a negative response, I'd say to myself, *Have the courage to face the truth!* That would motivate me to go ahead and find out what problems, objections, or negative responses people had.

Memorize this self-suggestion. Say it to yourself fifty times each morning and fifty times each afternoon for several days in a row. In time, you'll permanently program the concept into your "I Am" as a deep belief or value. This belief, when deeply formed, will then influence your emotions and actions. Every time you get in a situation where you need that reminder, the programming in your "I Am" will automatically send the command *Have the courage to face the truth!* to your "I Think" conscious mind. When that happens, act immediately by taking the appropriate actions.

Let me emphasize that this practice of self-suggestion can have a significant impact on your confidence and self-esteem. The key is to select statements that you'd like to become automatic habits, and then repeat them to yourself over a period of time.

Welcome and Understand Objections

When you ask a client, "What else should we discuss before making a decision now?" remember to practice the second Action Guide—Welcome and Understand Objections.

This step has been one of the most difficult ones for me to practice. Maybe it's human nature to want to ignore negative responses because it's so easy to personalize people's objections and unconsciously perceive that the person is rejecting us instead of our recommendations.

Welcoming objections isn't a normal response; it requires developing a strong emotional intelligence, which is one of the four core traits of high-achieving people.

Emotional intelligence grows within us as we do things that we fear or dislike. People who give in to their emotions and take the easy, undisciplined course in life's events have low emotional control. Many failures in selling come for this reason.

But salespeople can strengthen their emotional intelligence by doing activities, or practicing responses, that they'd rather not do.

In one of our courses, we teach salespeople the slogan *Go where you're afraid to go, do what you're afraid to do, and ask when you're afraid to ask.* Their assignment for a week is to practice this slogan and report back to the course members a week later. We hear many life-changing reports . . . salespeople call on higher-level decision makers than they've done before, new sales are made, and a new level of confidence is enjoyed when they practice the slogan.

Understanding Customers' Concerns Strengthens Rapport

Sincerely asking about people's feelings, concerns, or objections is in itself a form of reinforcement. The fact that you care enough to ask sends signals of your desire to serve them and create value for them. Your attempts to genuinely understand your clients' thoughts or concerns help you avoid head-on emotional or ego collisions. It removes barriers to communication and builds rapport.

As you work on understanding people's concerns, your success depends on your genuine desire to really know what they're thinking. Open listening is just that—open. It's devoid of bias or the need for a *comeback* that proves their concerns are unimportant or wrong.

Any attempts to change people's thinking usually causes them to strengthen their positions and become more rigid in their views. But if you value people's questions and concerns, they'll value your attempts to help them. Sincerely understanding your customers often helps them clarify their own thinking, and can even cause them to change their mind.

Identify and Isolate Specific Objections

As you welcome and understand customers' objections, you'll need to identify and isolate their real concerns and then deal with them. Here's how:

1. Ask questions to help you understand their concerns.
2. Listen without interrupting.
3. Repeat back to them your understanding of their concerns and get agreement that you've understood them correctly.

At this point, you'll often hear new concerns or objections. When you feel that a person's real interest is regressing, it may mean that you jumped to a negotiation position before they were truly sold on what you're presenting. If you see this happening, stop any negotiation strategy, go back, and get agreement on these important steps.

1. They have a need, are looking for a solution, and are willing to talk to you about one.
2. Your solution is what they want.
3. There's a sense of urgency in making a decision.
4. They truly have a problem and want to work through it.

At this point you'll often discover that your customer is either unconvinced that your solution is the best one for him or is reluctant to make a decision. You must find out what stage it is and go from there.

When you do, identify specific objections and get agreement that they can be worked through. If your customers still want what you're selling then it's time to move to the next step.

Discuss Possible Solutions—Ask Their Opinions for Best Solutions

Once people tell you, either verbally or with their actions, that they want what you're offering but still have concerns, it's time to discuss possible solutions. You can:

1. Ask for their opinions about the best solution.
2. Share your opinion about the best solution only when they'll be open to you.

Get your customers involved in solving their problems and working through their concerns. If they truly believe that you can satisfy their wants or needs, they should be as interested in working it out as you are.

Figuratively, this gets both of you on the same side of the bargaining table. This action prevents any adversarial relationship from occurring and strengthens your relationship with them. You emerge on a stronger partnership level.

Regardless of what you sell, this attitude will help you win customers.

Focus on Solutions Rather Than on Problems

Often when you get people to focus on possible solutions, they sell themselves. They work through their objections, fears, or hesitancy to buy.

I once worked with a person who had an unusual and successful way of avoiding arguments or allowing egos to torpedo the sale when problems arose.

Rather than allowing customers to focus only on the problem, she would say, "Okay, let's problem-solve! What are some possible solutions?"

As a result of gracefully getting customers to focus on solutions, she was able to avoid conflict and combativeness.

Remember this very important principle of negotiation—stay focused on solutions.

You'll learn that if you only *tell* people what the best solutions to their problems are, you'll rarely convince them or change their minds. *But when you ask their opinions* about possible solutions, you stand a far greater chance of a successful negotiation.

People are much more apt to act on their ideas than on yours, so try to steer the conversation away from the problems or objections, and instead seek joint solutions.

I know that this doesn't always work. Some people are unyielding and won't give an inch. But I believe that most people will respond positively to your efforts; if they don't, you probably wouldn't want them as customers anyway.

Negotiating with Different Behavior Styles

As you negotiate problems and objections with people, you'll want to remember these simple guidelines about different Behavior Styles:

1. Talkers need personal support and help as they work toward a decision.
2. Doers want to be convinced of results and make their own decisions.
3. Controllers want facts and documentation.
4. Supporters want plenty of information and time to make a decision.

Try to think of some typical objections that you'll receive from different styles of people.

Concerns Talkers Will Have

The Talker might object by saying:

- *"I'll have to see how the others feel about this."*
- *"I'll want to be careful not to offend anyone with my decision."*
- *"Give me more time to make a decision."*
- *"I'll have to sell this idea to some other people."*

Talkers like to buy from people they like. Their biggest problem is deciding which person to buy from when they like two or more salespeople. This fear is revealed by statements like "My cousin is really going to be mad at me if I buy from you!"

Talkers often have to get financial approval from others, either in their companies or from their spouses. You'll hear statements like "Okay, well, let me see if I can come up with the money" or "Let me talk it over with so-and-so."

Talkers' objections or problems center around these facts:

- *When it comes to money, they often have to get final approval from others.*
- *They fear social disapproval in making decisions.*
- *They have conflicts when two or more sellers are competing.*
- *They want to make sure that everyone's happy with their decisions.*

Doers' Concerns

Doers' objections are quite different. Typically, Doers don't have problems making decisions. Usually, they enjoy making them. Nor are they overly swayed by fear of social disapproval. They're more concerned with getting results, or getting the job done, than with how satisfied other people are. A strong Doer ruffles feathers and often rushes in where angels fear to tread. They make decisions and sometimes jam them down other people's throats.

Doers will often object by saying:

- *"I'm not totally convinced that this'll work."*
- *"I think I can get a better deal than you're offering me."*
- *"Who else has made this work?"*
- *"We've got to have a faster delivery date."*

Controllers' Concerns

Controllers' concerns arise when they feel they don't have enough data or proof that your product or service is indeed what they need. They want facts, figures, and supporting data. You must satisfy their accuracy-driven, organized, logical minds before they'll make decisions. You'll hear these types of questions or objections from Controllers:

- *"You haven't provided me with enough accurate data."*
- *"I'm not convinced that you can guarantee the quality."*
- *"We'd prefer not to buy until we see a successful installation that you've done for another firm."*
- *"I'm unclear on your specifications or warranty."*

Controllers will object until they're sure your product or service will give them their desired return on investment.

Supporters' Concerns

Supporters' objections will center on these concerns:

- *"Don't rush me . . . I don't want to make hasty decisions."*
- *"I don't want to run any big risks."*
- *"I want to take plenty of time and make sure I'm getting the best price and just the right product."*
- *"I want to make sure I understand everything before making a decision."*

Common objections from Supporters are:

- *"We've never done it like that before."*
- *"We've always used red widgets and now you're trying to sell us yellow ones."*
- *"We've done business with your competition for twenty-nine years and I don't see any reason to change now."*

Supporters will also give many variations of "I've got to think about it more" or "I'll have to sleep on it. . . . I never make a snap decision."

Like Controllers, Supporters want lots of details about your product or service features. But while Controllers want to know how it's made for the sake of knowing how it'll perform, Supporters want to know how it's made for the sake of pure knowledge. There's a big difference.

How to Know When You've Completed the Negotiation Step

1. People want your product or service if their concerns can be worked through.
2. You've identified their concerns or objections.
3. You understand what each person wants from the transaction.
4. You've successfully worked through all their concerns or objections.

How to Gain the Most from This Chapter

Read this chapter three times this week, making notes in the margins. Write the Negotiation Action Guides on an index card. Carry it with you and refer to it several times each day this next week. Practice the guides whenever you have a chance.

Whenever you think you're ready to negotiate, ask yourself these questions:

1. *Do I have strong rapport with the customer or customers?*
2. *Have I identified their real wants or needs?*
3. *Have they admitted that these are their real wants or needs?*
4. *Have they agreed that they want to fill or satisfy these wants or needs?*
5. *Have they agreed to work with me in filling their wants or needs?*
6. *Do I fully understand any concerns or objections they have?*
7. *Have I paraphrased their concerns back to them?*
8. *Do they agree that they want to work this concern out?*
9. *Have I asked their opinion about how to work out their concerns?*
10. *Have we reached a successful resolution?*

Asking and answering these questions can help you know where you are on a transaction. Often you discover that you haven't accomplished previous AID,Inc. steps.

Remember that successful negotiation isn't a strategy—it's a win-win attitude that's focused on helping customers make the best, most informed decisions.

[11]

Conditioning Your Mind for Unlimited Prosperity Consciousness

I've learned a lot about prosperity consciousness from my friend and current business partner, John Teets. John grew up in a blue-collar family in a town outside Chicago. His main asset was an incredibly high desire to succeed. In his late teens, he got into the food service business, and because of his work ethic and abilities, he caught the attention of a wealthy person who helped finance his large restaurant, skating rink, and shopping center.

Although highly successful at a young age, he experienced one year that left him emotionally, spiritually, and financially devastated. His young wife suddenly died of an aneurysm, his business burned to the ground, and his brother was killed in a construction accident.

To deal with his devastating losses, he began a continuing pattern of self-improvement. He took a Dale Carnegie course. He read great self-help books like *Think and Grow Rich, The Magic of Believing, Psycho-Cybernetics, The Magic of Thinking Big,* and others. But he didn't just read them as many people do. *He pulled out success principles and applied them* to his life. He learned to feed his subconscious with goals and repeated affirmations. He wrote his goals on cards and looked at them several times a day.

While weathering these dark periods, he developed new strengths and emerged with a compelling resolve to achieve very high goals. And he did, becoming chairman of The Dial Corp., then a Fortune 100 company.

After retiring a few years ago, he now enjoys a very prosperous lifestyle. He has his own Jet Star II business jet, a beautiful home on the Pebble Beach Golf Course, and the finest single collection of Napoleon-era French clocks in existence. More important, his life has great balance—family, business, and a strong religious faith.

As I've listened to him tell of his climb in the corporate world, I've been struck by the core strategy he used to reach the success he now enjoys. He learned to feed his goals and build himself at his subconscious level, through affirmations and daily mental exercises. In Integrity Selling language, he planted prosperity beliefs in his "I Am," and saw them materialize into their tangible form. As his "I Am" grew and continually expanded, his external success grew proportionally.

He had learned the *source* of prosperity.

And you can, too.

Prosperity Consciousness Defined

Prosperity consciousness is a state of mind that expects good things to happen in the future. It's filled with faith, hope, joy, optimism, forgiveness, and gratitude.

"Truly, thoughts are things; and powerful things at that, when they are mixed with definiteness of purpose, persistence, and a burning desire for the translation into riches, or other material objects," wrote Napoleon Hill in his classic, *Think and Grow Rich.*

A poverty consciousness is a mind state that expects bad things to happen. It's characterized by doubts, fear, anxiety, and low expectations.

Each of us has a prosperity or poverty consciousness programmed within our "I Am" dimension—to varying degrees. But once the programming is set, our powerful Goal-Seeking Mechanism then continuously works to convert our programming into its tangible equivalent. Our inner thoughts, beliefs, and expectations are silently yet powerfully translated into actual realities. "The thing I feared has come upon me," the prophet Job wrote, stating a psychological truth.

Your actual sustained sales will be subconsciously engineered so they're consistent with your inner beliefs or expectations—the degree of your prosperity or poverty consciousness. Regardless of how intelligent you are, how great a product you have, what kind of market you have, over time your sales will be consistent with the expectations of your inner consciousness.

I've said this many times in this book. I continue to learn it on different levels, as every student of success does.

The Source of Prosperity

The source, the wellspring, the cause of your personal success and prosperity isn't your knowledge, the quality of your product, or service superiority, or even market conditions. It's something else. Over time, I've learned that people who possess a strong internal "prosperity consciousness" consistently do well. Yes, they also experience temporary bumps in the road, but in the larger view, they do well.

As a salesperson intent on achieving higher levels of success—in sales and customer loyalty—you must treat yourself as three people. You must learn to properly nurture and feed these three parts that make up the one you: your "I Think," your "I Feel," and your "I Am."

It's with your "I Think" that you use willpower to perform functions that are routine and maybe even redundant. Doing things you fear. Doing things that bore you. Successful selling demands that you be disciplined and detailed.

This logical-versus-emotional tug-of-war is in itself enough to keep you feeling pulled in directions you don't like or understand. And if you go too far in the direction of either of these, your productivity suffers. You must maintain a balance between what you know and how you feel.

The fact that you've chosen the sales field is probably proof that you tend to lean more toward the emotional than logical side. You probably enjoy interacting with people over processing details. You value acceptance from people, and the thrill of making a sale can seem to validate your worth. Most of us who sell have a high need for recognition, and this need drives us. Successful selling answers this need.

Feelings Overrule Logic

Your "I Feel" reigns supreme over your "I Think." As I mentioned before, in a contest your "I Feel" will win out, on average, 85 percent of the time. Selling is mostly emotional—from identifiable ones like confidence or fear, to more subtle ones like feelings of worthiness. These internal emotions can powerfully influence your activity levels and then your actual sales.

But it's the programming in your "I Am" dimension that triggers these emotions when facing different situations. It's your perception of who you are, what you're capable of achieving, what level of sales are possible for you to make, what level of people you're able to relate to and call on. Your deep unconscious beliefs determine what kind of lifestyle you deserve to have. All these and other unconscious assumptions are firmly planted in your "I Am," and they rule your life from behind the veils of consciousness.

Willpower, knowledge, discipline, and intentions alone will eventually fail you, because they haven't the sustaining power to withstand strong emotional demands that selling makes. But emotional pull without discipline and self-control can lead you to inactivity, unless deeper values, beliefs, and character keep you balanced.

Simply stated, since you're actually three people rolled into one, you must learn to balance these dimensions and use each part in an effective, contributing manner. You must balance:

1. Your willpower, discipline, and knowledge, with
2. Your emotions and feelings, which are being triggered by
3. Your values, self-beliefs, and character.

Strengthening this balance will then lead you into higher levels of personal fulfillment, sales success, and true prosperity. In a real sense, the Action Guides in this book are designed to help you strengthen this balance—when you practice them.

Don't Be Daunted by This Journey

Again, I want to remind you that conditioning your mind for unlimited prosperity consciousness will not be easy; but you can do it if you desire it enough.

It doesn't happen overnight. Building yourself at your "I Am" dimension is a lifelong commitment, since it holds the key to this balance. You'll learn that the room for self-improvement grows larger as you walk farther into it. As this journey progresses, you'll see more possibilities for even greater self-improvement.

High achievers choose to continually focus and think about:

1. Creating the most value for the most people, and
2. Knowing that they'll be rewarded in proportion to the value they create.

Prosperity-Development Strategies

There are some powerful strategies that will work wonders for you as you program your "I Am" with them. Before I explain specific prosperity-development strategies, though, let me emphasize a basic principle: *Plant success-producing beliefs in your "I Am," and in time you'll see these beliefs transformed into their tangible equivalent.*

Beliefs firmly planted in your "I Am" will eventually influence your actions, feelings, abilities, and behaviors. They'll give you a stronger sense of direction and purpose. They'll also form the picture of who you'll become. "Dream lofty dreams," wrote James Allen in his classic, *As a Man Thinketh*, "and as you dream, so shall you become."

Let's stop a moment and go back to the beginning—which you'll often do as you move through different success levels.

Begin with Goal Clarity

Your journey to greater prosperity begins with strong goal clarity—establishing specific goals that:

1. You truly want to reach
2. You believe are possible for you to reach
3. You feel worthy to enjoy

Set mostly short-range goals, ones that you can reach in a few weeks or months and are just a bit beyond where you're currently performing. Begin with six goals in specific areas like: sales, income (if applicable), family, spirituality, education, finance, personal improvement, and so on. Make sure they're measurable and that each describes a desired end result. Answer *where, what, when, why, who,* and *how,* as you define your strategy for stronger prosperity consciousness.

Transfer these goals to a card or pocket folder that you can carry with you. Take it out and read it several times each day. Feed them to your inner Goal-Seeking Mechanism—part of your "I Am"—by focusing on each goal and its accompanying rewards several times each day.

Feed Your Goal-Seeking Mechanism

After setting these six goals, drop any concern about whether you can reach them or not. Instead, every time you read or think about your goals, consciously dwell on the rewards you'll enjoy when you reach them. Suspend logic for the moment and fully enjoy fantasizing about the gratification you'll enjoy when the goals are reached. Since a goal is something that hasn't happened yet, logic can dampen your beliefs. Only your emotional desire for rewards will carry you through.

When you discover, as you will from time to time, that a goal is either unrealistic or unimportant to you, immediately delete or change it. Revise your list of six, and continue feeding them to your "I Am" by reading them over and over and focusing on the rewards you'll enjoy when you reach them.

To help build belief in your "I Am," cut out pictures or graphic symbols that remind you of your goals. Keep them in front of you. Look at them several times each day. Every time you look, visualize yourself enjoying their reality.

After twenty-one days have passed, you'll begin to notice some subtle changes within yourself. You'll develop an inner belief that your goals are indeed possible for you to reach. Keep up the daily programming. As you whet your appetite for your goals, you'll automatically increase your inner motivation to achieve them.

As your motivation builds, your inner Goal-Seeking Mechanism will begin to steer you to your desired goals. You'll have sudden hunches, insights, or ideas. You'll wake up in the middle of the night with the answer to questions you've struggled with popping into your mind. You'll mysteriously discover people, places, or things that will aid your goal achievement. You'll stumble over resources, knowledge, or other support that you probably wouldn't have recognized without a goal. Once you discover the reality of your creative Goal-Seeking Mechanism, barriers will fall and whole new levels of prosperity consciousness will automatically grow in your "I Am."

This increased prosperity consciousness will cause you to believe more in your success possibilities and set higher goals that will lead you into a lifetime of higher achievement.

Cultivating an Abundance Awareness

When I was a teenager, I lived with my mother, father, and two sisters in a small four-room house on the outskirts of a small West Texas oil town. We had no streetlights, sidewalks, lawn, or paved drive. My bedroom was in the small kitchen; my small rollaway bed had to be folded up before breakfast and the chrome dinette had to be shoved into a corner before I could open up my bed at night.

I was deeply embarrassed and didn't want the kids at school to know where we lived. I never understood why my father had settled for this level of living. Nor did I understand his reasoning that, in essence, said, *Willinghams have always been poor*. He believed that we should live on that level; he settled for it.

I vowed that when I grew up I'd get an education and be very successful. Later, I learned that poverty and prosperity are attitude. People hold beliefs about what's possible for them to enjoy or earn. Every one of us has some picture painted in our unconscious "I Am" that motivates our actions, expectations, and decisions.

Because of my hunger to enjoy a higher degree of prosperity, I eventually picked up my first self-help book, *Success Through a Positive Mental Attitude*. I read it six or seven times before I began to understand it. The message that Napoleon Hill and W. Clement Stone delivered was *Whatever the mind of man can conceive and believe, it can achieve*.

After several months of digesting the book, I was able to convert the message from a neat little rhyme to a foundational success principle. In time, I designed a self-suggestion: *God has created everything in abundance; I only have to reach out and claim that which can be mine!* I said this to myself over and over each day, until I began to believe it in the deepest parts of my "I Am."

Then my life began to change.

Suggestion, Self-Suggestion, Autosuggestion

To understand the process I used to pull myself up by my bootstraps, it's important to understand three concepts. They are: *suggestion*, *self-suggestion*, and *autosuggestion*.

A *suggestion* is anything that comes into your consciousness that creates an impact. The suggestion may be in the form of words, pictures, or other sensory inputs. You're being subjected to suggestions all the time—through television, newspapers, radio, and other mediums.

Self-suggestion is the act of consciously choosing statements that you'd like to describe you and then suggesting these thoughts through words you say to yourself. When you repeat the words to yourself, over a period of time, you'll eventually *believe* or *accept* them as fact. The key is repetition and time lapse.

Understanding this dynamic function of the mind can give you a clue to changing the way you think and live. For instance, if you want to develop a new positive thought pattern, belief, or value, you can use *self-suggestion* by consciously repeating the desired attitude fifty times in the morning and fifty times in the evening.

If you keep this up for at least three to four weeks, you'll begin to subconsciously *believe* what you've suggested. At this point, your subconscious "I Am" has basically *bought* the idea or thought if it's consistent with your values. Your new beliefs in your "I Am" will then influence your emotions and subsequent actions and keep them consistent with your inner programming.

Autosuggestion occurs when your subconscious "I Am" has accepted an idea or thought. It *automatically* flashes these thoughts to your conscious "I Think" when you need them. Then it's up to you to take appropriate action.

Let me give you an example. Early in my adult life, I discovered that I thoroughly enjoyed procrastinating. Whenever I saw something that needed to be done, I'd put it off. It got me into a lot of trouble.

Practicing what I had read in *Success Through a Positive Mental Attitude*, I began to say to myself fifty times in the morning and fifty times in the evening, "When I see something that needs to be done, I do it!"

After a few weeks of saying this to myself each day, a strange thing began to happen. Every time I saw something that needed to be done, this thought, "When I see something that needs to be done, I do it!" would *automatically* flash from my subconscious "I Am" to my conscious "I Think." I'd find myself responding with action—doing the thing that needed to be done.

Now that you understand *suggestion*, *self-suggestion*, and *autosuggestion*, let me encourage you to take some time and write down up to six self-suggestions—statements that describe behaviors or attitudes you'd like to have or be doing now. State them in the present tense. For example: "I weigh 170 pounds!" "I eat to live, rather than live to eat!"

Learn from High Achievers

Here's a powerful success principle: Find people who are achieving the level of success that you'd like to enjoy, and learn from them. As you read this, you may be tempted to ask, "But why would a highly successful person be willing to spend time with me?"

Good question. Here's something I've learned about highly successful people: *They have a strong need to perpetuate their success, so they're usually quite willing to share ideas with people who sincerely want to learn from them.* In addition, most highly successful people owe their beginning to one or two other high achievers who mentored them. Helping you is a way of paying back the people who helped them on their way up.

I remember meeting Dr. Maxwell Maltz, author of *Psycho-Cybernetics*, in 1968, working with him, and learning from him until he passed away in 1975. I asked to become his student, and promised to do my best to pass along his *Psycho-Cybernetics* teachings. At the time I met him, I was just getting my training and development business going. He had achieved world renown with his classic book. He saw me as a willing learner, and spent many hours with me in our hundred or so visits.

I paid for all my own travel expenses as I worked with him, and asked nothing from him except the chance to learn about human behavior. He was quite willing to grant this to me.

There have been other high achievers from whom I've asked to learn. In almost all cases, they were delighted to help me. I consider this book and the courses I develop a way of paying them back.

Feast Your Eyes on Beauty and Good Design

I've talked about this before, but you'll understand it deeper while you learn about developing a "prosperity consciousness." Spend time studying beauty and good design. Observe good architecture, art, upscale products, homes, landscapes, fashions, and restaurant menus. Notice what highly successful people wear, and how they groom themselves.

I learned to listen more deeply to people to see if I could understand how the subjects of their conversation might reveal their level of prosperity consciousness—their expectations and views of their own possibilities.

One of my favorite questions to ask people was "What are some things that helped you get where you are today?" The responses are enlightening.

I love to go to art galleries, to design studios, and into beautiful buildings. I've developed the habit of emotionally observing this beauty and good design in almost an unconscious way—by inhaling it into my mind.

As I do these activities, I constantly tell myself, "What I feed my mind, I'll become!"

It's not that I want to buy these things; rather, I want to allow their beauty or masterful design to saturate my senses.

What You Feed Your Mind, You'll Become

What you feed your mind, you'll become is a universal success principle.

Since we all have choices of what we think about, where we go, what we do with our time, and whom we spend it with, we chart our own courses and construct our own mental and emotional paradigms. Successful people choose to feed their minds on beauty, truth, abundance, or wholesome things. Do you choose to be around people with positive, loving, moral, wholesome energy? Or, by default, do you choose people with negative, cynical, and depressing energy? In both cases, your mind will be fed.

The thoughts, associations, and outer behaviors you choose with your "I Think" are immediately filtered through your "I Am" to produce emotions in your "I Feel." Your "I Am" is your spiritual part that houses your values and your sense of right and wrong, called "the Spirit of Wisdom" by Dr. Carl Jung.

Negative choices and associations tend to weaken your "I Am" dimension, creating stress and reducing energy. Positive thoughts, choices, actions, and associations are always inspiring and energizing. As the apostle Paul wrote in Philippians 4:8, New International Version:

> *Whatever is true, whatever is noble, whatever is right, whatever is pure, whatever is lovely, whatever is admirable—if anything is excellent or praiseworthy—think about such things.*

This is excellent psychology, and a pathway to abundance, wholeness, happiness, and creative living.

You'll become what you feed your mind. And your actions, responses, and behaviors spring forth from this, influencing your long-term sales success more than your knowledge, sales skills, products or services, or market conditions.

Please understand that I'm not suggesting that all people who make a lot of money are successfully balanced. Some of the most unhappy people in the world have monetary wealth but lack fulfilling relationships, self-respect, or a sense of spiritual significance.

But if you carefully feed your mind on what you eventually want to become, focusing on more than monetary gain, your inner beliefs will begin to translate themselves into their physical equivalent.

How to Gain the Most from This Chapter

Read this chapter over at least three times this week. Study the concepts and suggestions, and pick out a couple to focus on.

Pay special attention to the section on *Suggestion, Self-suggestion,* and *Autosuggestion.* Do the exercise I described. Design six of your own self-suggestions, and write them on index cards. Describe who you want to be, goals you want to reach, or how you want to perform at a point in the future. Read them three times each day. Repeat them to yourself.

Each time you repeat a self-suggestion, immediately visualize yourself already being, having, or possessing that trait. Picture how it would help you. Anticipate how it will feel when you've developed it. Pre-enjoy the victory.

Pick out highly successful people from whom you'd like to learn. Go to them and tell them that you'd like to learn from them. Assure them that you'll practice what they share with you, and that you'll pass on what you learn to others. You'll find this to be a great experience. But a word of advice: Always play the student. Listen. Talk only to ask questions and later to report on your practice.

Set aside an hour each week to feast your eyes on beauty, good design, or abundance. Analyze these things and try to understand what makes them stand out. Allow their beauty or elegance to saturate your senses.

And, finally, say to yourself over and over each day: *What I feed my mind, I'll become!* You'll find that this self-suggestion will be planted in your "I Am" through time lapse and repetition. As you begin to understand the power of your own self-suggestions, you'll be able to more carefully choose your words, actions, relationships, the places you go, people you're around, and what you do—knowing that all these are being fed directly to your "I Am."

Remember . . . *What you feed your mind, you'll become.* This powerful, eternal truth can lead you to increased abundance and personal fulfillment.

[12]

Close: Get a Positive Decision That Creates Mutual Value for You and Your Customers

INTEGRITY SELLING SUCCESS PRINCIPLE

**You don't sell in the close,
you close after you've sold.**

Almost nothing about selling has been more misunderstood, maligned, or mistaken than the closing step.

When closing is taught as a strategy to win at the expense of customers, whether your product or service is right for them or not, it flies in the face of Integrity Selling.

Closing or finalizing a transaction should be viewed as an attitude rather than as a strategy. A strategy is a salesperson-focused activity, designed to get people to say "yes." An attitude is "If this is the best solution for the customer, I should help him make the right decision."

In this chapter, you'll learn what integrity closing really is, how and when it's done, and what attitude or ethical intent drives it.

What Is Closing?

Closing is simply asking for a decision or a closing action when a person is ready to say "yes." You don't sell in the close, you close after you've made a sale. You don't ask for a decision until after:

1.   You've understood your customers' needs or wants.
2.   You've offered a solution that they like and want.
3.   You've worked through any problems or concerns they may have.
4.   You've agreed on terms, price, or delivery time.

In other words, you've completed these AID,Inc. steps: You've

1.   Approached
2.   Interviewed
3.   Demonstrated
4.   Validated
5.   Negotiated

When these steps have been completed, if your customers haven't already suggested a closing action (which they often do), it's time for you to ask for one.

When you get a negative response, it's proof that one or more of these five steps wasn't properly completed. In this chapter, I'll explain what you can do when you do get a negative closing response.

The Closing Action Guides

1.   Ask trial-closing questions to get opinions and response.
2.   Listen to and reinforce each response.

3. Restate how the benefits will outweigh the costs.
4. Ask for a decision.

Ask Trial-Closing Questions to Get Opinions and Responses

Trial-closing questions ask for *opinions*. Closing questions ask for *decisions*. There's a big difference.

When customers talk and you listen, it creates the best sales environment you can structure. So consciously ask opinion questions during your Demonstration, Validation, and Negotiation steps.

When you think you've successfully progressed to the point where a customer says, "Yes, I want what you have and believe it will fill my needs," it's time to ask trial-closing questions.

It's not uncommon for you to think your customers are ready to make a decision, only to find out that they really aren't. I've made this mistake many times. Sudden fears pop up; they need approval from someone they didn't tell me about earlier. Sometimes I'm just more anxious to move the sale along than they are.

I'm always amazed at how people's minds can suddenly become less positive as decision time nears.

You'll discover that trial-closing, or opinion, questions can be asked when:

1. You're not sure you know all their feelings or concerns, or
2. You think you know them, but negatives suddenly pop up.

Here are some general trial-closing questions:

- *What other questions or concerns do you have that we need to discuss before making a decision?*
- *At this point, what have I failed to explain?*
- *Who might have some decision input that we haven't gotten agreement from?*

- *At this point, do you clearly see how the benefits of my solution outweigh the costs to you?*
- *Would you explain your decision process or criteria again?*
- *At this point, do you need more validation or evidence of the benefits I can give you?*

Listen to and Reinforce Each Response

As you ask trial-closing questions and get opinions and responses, you'll want to give positive reinforcement.

You can do this in several ways. You give positive reinforcement every time you acknowledge what people tell you—any time you let them know that you listened to them and heard what they said. You can acknowledge or give feedback to people by nodding approval, by verbalizing agreement, by paraphrasing what they tell you, and by using gestures that show you heard what they said.

Why should you perform these actions?

First, remembering to do these actions forces you to really listen and remember what customers tell you. Second, it proves to them that you listened and remembered what they said. Third, it influences even deeper levels of customer persuasion. It heightens rapport and trust, and lowers their natural resistance to decide.

Listening Fills People's Needs

One of the greatest psychological needs people have is for other people to listen to them without bias, and without waiting for a chance to argue a point or jump in and resume talking.

When you fulfill this need in others, they'll often unconsciously want to fulfill your needs. They'll begin to listen to you without bias or resistance. *Asking questions and listening to opinions is a powerful method of persuasion.*

When you do this kind of total, in-depth listening, you're going to learn what your customers or prospects are thinking. They're going to give you plenty of clues. When you've had positive clues as to what a person's decision will be, then and only then is it time to ask for a decision.

But I'll be honest . . . there will be times when you think you know someone's thoughts or concerns but you don't. A whole new objection that has been kept well hidden before may suddenly pop out. Usually when this happens, you'll find that you haven't completed a prior AID,Inc. step. Your customers' objections or indecision may give you these insights:

- *You didn't understand their needs completely . . . or you didn't Interview well enough.*
- *You didn't Demonstrate how your product or service will fill their needs.*
- *You didn't Validate the purchase.*
- *You didn't Negotiate to reach an acceptable solution.*
- *They either can't make a decision, or have no sense of urgency.*

Negative Response at Closing May Reveal Your Interview Wasn't Completed

Not long ago, I worked with a major company to design a training program. Several months had gone by, lots of work had been done, several meetings took place, terms were negotiated, and contracts were drawn. Everything had been approved and was ready to sign.

After all this time had elapsed, after I thought all the bases had been covered, out of the clear blue, the chief decision maker looked at me and said, "But this isn't what I want!" I was stunned, as were all the other people. "What do you want?" I asked.

"I don't know," she replied, "but this isn't it." Then she walked out of the conference room.

It dawned on me that I hadn't completed the Interview step several weeks earlier. I hadn't anticipated that this person would do a "180" on her decision. I wasn't able to save the sale.

Think for a moment about responses you sometimes get just when you're about to Close. Responses like "I've got to look around" show that you didn't Interview, Demonstrate, or Validate well. "I need to get approval from others" shows that you didn't find out who the decision makers were in your Interview.

Responses like "It's too much money" tell that you didn't negotiate well, didn't demonstrate the value in your offering, or didn't understand their budget.

Instead of combatively trying to change someone's mind, you should identify the step you missed and attempt to complete it. Sometimes you can, other times you can't.

Restate How the Benefits Will Outweigh the Costs

When you believe that all concerns have been addressed, and that it's time to ask for a decision, you'll want to bring the conversation into a logical focus by restating how the benefits will outweigh the costs.

Remember that before people buy or agree to anything, they must first weigh the benefits against the cost. When I use the word "cost," I mean more than just money. "Costs" include time, risk involved, political issues, and resistance to change.

Before you ask for a decision, make sure that the person truly believes that the value outweighs the cost. Also, in selling with integrity, you'll want to be convinced, yourself, that the value to them exceeds their cost. If it doesn't, you shouldn't want them to have what you're selling.

These actions and attitudes will strongly impact your closing in two ways. First, they'll ensure that you focus more on the benefits of your product instead of the features. Second, they'll help you stay aware of all the elements included in the cost to your customer. Ensuring that the benefits outweigh the cost will help you see things from their viewpoint, and, in turn, help them see things from your viewpoint.

Ask for a Decision

When you get positive feedback to your trial-close questions, all concerns seem to have been successfully worked through, and you think it's time to close, you can simply ask for a decision. Remember, the Integrity Selling definition of closing is simply asking for a decision at the right time.

When you're sure of the value you can create for people, and they're also convinced that it exceeds the cost you're asking, you should ask for the appropriate closing action. This may include getting a purchase order, a check, or a contract signed.

Always remember that people with different behavior styles will make their decisions in very distinct ways.

How Talkers Make Decisions

Talkers will not make logical decisions based on facts and information; their decisions to buy will be based more on feelings. They'll often find it difficult to turn you down or reject you. They probably won't come right out with a "no," but will stall or make excuses.

More than any other style, Talkers prefer to buy from people whom they like and trust. They're greatly influenced by the people they buy from and may be swayed by people with enthusiastic, strong personalities.

Before you can expect a decision from a Talker, you often need other people involved. Many Talkers want help when making decisions.

Remember that a Talker needs social acceptance, and that need will dominate their buying process.

How Doers Make Decisions

Doers are usually ready to make quick decisions once they believe that your solution will give them the bottom-line results they want. If you've done the Validation and Negotiation steps well, you can quickly and directly ask Doers to buy. In fact, they'll often tell you to move ahead before you ask.

Be sure to take as many details off their shoulders as possible.

Doers want you to be confident that you can give them the benefits they want, and will be influenced by your confidence. They like for you to be direct with them, so don't stall or be wishy-washy.

Pressuring a Doer will usually backfire. Their egos won't allow you to win them over if they feel like you're trying to push them into a decision. You must yield to their strong personalities and allow the buying decision to be their own idea.

How Controllers Make Decisions

Before you ask Controllers for a decision, you must ensure that they have all the facts. They'll have no trouble making decisions once they feel they have all the facts, and they won't be swayed by emotions.

Make sure that you've discussed the risks involved. Don't try to *minimize* the risks, just show how the risks are outweighed by the benefits. Controllers respect salespeople who clearly spell out the downside of things. Always ask Controllers, "Is there any other information I can get for you before you make a decision?"

Controllers don't like to be pressured—they'll coolly cut you off and send you on your way. When you ask them for a decision, be direct. If they're not ready to make a decision, ask them when they will be. They'll usually honor the time frames they commit to.

How Supporters Make Decisions

When you're working with Supporters, remember that they don't like change or taking risks. You can expect them to be slow in making buying decisions. They'll want to "sleep on it," or take the time to think things through.

Supporters often need help in making decisions. They want to please other people with their purchases, so they'll want to be convinced of your product's safety and security before making decisions. It's so important that *you* understand their perceived risks so you can reassure them before asking for a purchase decision.

You'll confuse Supporters if you put pressure on them. Pressure makes them more indecisive. But when you give them time and follow up with them, your closings will increase significantly.

What Do You Do When Customers Say "No"?

If you've sold products or services for very long, you've probably discovered that there are times when you think you've done everything right but you still get a negative final decision. After all, people aren't always logical.

When this happens, you must try to discover whether:

1. It's a closed case with no chance of reopening, or
2. There's a chance of working out a solution with continued dialogue.

I have had numerous situations occur where my solution was rejected, only to find out that there were some misunderstandings or miscommunications with prospective clients. I've also lost sales, only to be called back in when the competitive programs that were purchased instead didn't give customers their expected results.

When you think you've accomplished all the AID,Inc. steps correctly and you get a negative decision, you must determine if there's a chance of their reconsidering. Often, you discover that your customer has already purchased the item from a competitor, and it will be years before they purchase another automobile (or whatever you're selling).

When you find yourself at a dead end, it's time to be gracious, thank the people involved for the opportunity to work with them, wish them the best, and ask if you can stay in touch.

When you do determine that their decision or purchases have not been made, and they're still interested, you must get permission to ask more questions so you can understand where they are, what the delay was, and how they want you to respond.

Keep remembering that all purchases aren't made from a purely logical base. This is true at every step of AID,Inc., but especially in the close step.

Re-entry Questions

Often I thought I understood people's needs, offered a solution they liked, cleared up any concerns, and was confident my prospective customer was ready to commit to a decision, only to receive a "no" from them.

Complete about-faces can happen suddenly, leaving you wondering, "Are they the same people who've been so positive until now?"

If the door to a sale hasn't been completely closed, you'll want to ask a general question: "Where do you want to go from here?" The answer will give you an indicator of interest and openness.

When customers leave an opening for further discussion, here are some types of questions you might ask:

1. "Do you still have the same need that we've previously discussed?"
2. "Was my solution what you wanted?"
3. "Have I proven that I can give you the benefits you want?"
4. "Have I misinterpreted your level of interest?"
5. "Have I misunderstood your urgency in making a decision?"
6. "Have we brought everyone into our conversations that we need to?"
7. "Are you looking at another product or service solution?"
8. "Do we have a problem with pricing issues or terms of sale?"
9. "Have questions or concerns popped into your mind that we haven't discussed before?"
10. "What can I do at this point to best serve you?"

Many sales have been pulled out of the fire because of the salesperson's ability to ask questions and help customers sort out what they want.

Customer's Fear of Making Decisions

In the real world of selling, you'll encounter many people who are eager and excited about your products or service—until decision time comes. Then the fear of making a wrong decision suddenly overwhelms them. People's emotions can completely change when they reach this decision point. The changes can be so radical and abrupt that you'll wonder, "Where is the logic in all this?"

Human nature can cause customers to be friendly, open, and seemingly very positive and receptive to your solutions. But the closer you get to a decision point, an inner tension, or in Dr. Leon Festinger's words, a *cognitive dissonance*, is aroused that can cause people to resort to strange behaviors.

Some Behavior Styles experience *cognitive dissonance*, while others don't feel this inner tension as decision time approaches.

Look at this model.

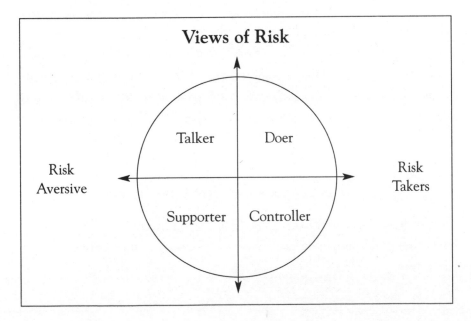

Here are typical behaviors you can expect as you near decision time with people:

1. Talkers will experience high cognitive dissonance if they think that their popularity or social acceptance is at risk.
2. Doers will experience little or no cognitive dissonance when they're convinced of results. In fact, once convinced of the results they'll enjoy, they'll often push you to a close.
3. Supporters will experience high internal conflicts when pressure is applied or risks haven't been removed.
4. Controllers will experience inner conflicts when your proof or evidence hasn't convinced them of the efficacy of your offering.

Often by patiently drawing out people's feelings, you can help them overcome their internal conflict of making a decision. Your genuine desire to understand their feelings will help them move to a more comfortable level and go ahead with a decision.

At this point, any pressure you apply further confuses most people and makes it more difficult to move ahead.

For many people, the fear of making a wrong decision will override their perceived benefits of making one. Their emotional state will almost always need your patience, concern, and understanding. Often when you respond to people in this way, you help them move past fear and make good decisions.

Salespeople's Closing Conflicts

Not only do customers experience illogical, emotional conflicts at decision time; salespeople do too. These conflicts can range between these extremes:

1. The hard closer who isn't afraid to ask, who applies too much pressure, doesn't really care about people's needs, only wants to fill his own need to make a sale.
2. The weak closer who is reluctant to ask for decisions, is more concerned with being rejected, and would rather lose a sale than face the possible "no."

Obviously, neither of these extremes is correct. Both create conflicts for salespeople. The "hard closer" loses sales by alienating people. The "weak closer" alienates himself from the truth.

My associates and I have also seen many salespeople approaching a close suddenly freeze up, unable to move further.

This strange phenomenon is caused by several factors:

1. They view selling as getting people to do things for them, and they don't feel comfortable asking.
2. They need the sales so badly that they aren't focusing on the value they can give customers, creating conflicts within them.
3. Their low self-esteem doesn't allow them to profit from other people.

As with customers, salespeople also can experience *cognitive dissonance,* or mental or emotional conflicts when the time comes to ask for decisions.

Cognitive dissonance can happen when salespeople:

1. Don't believe the value of their offering exceeds the cost to the customer.
2. Feel that closing is getting the customer to do something for them, rather than them doing something for the customer.
3. View selling as an unprofessional activity.

4. Fear rejection too strongly.
5. Have feelings of low self-worth.
6. Need to make a sale more than they want to help customers.

Think about the Sales Congruence Model I presented in Chapter 3. You'll remember that when those five dimensions are in conflict, stress is created, sales will be lower, and *cognitive dissonance* is the result.

People with a "poverty consciousness" have a difficult time closing because they don't believe they should earn more than they've been earning. As an example, I've talked to many salespeople who unconsciously didn't think they should earn more than their father did. The idea of being more financially successful than their father created a *cognitive dissonance* within them.

"I Don't Need to Make This Sale!"

Overcoming the *need to make a sale* isn't always easy. But if you're going to earn a living as a salesperson, you're going to have to make sales. I've discovered that the more I need to make a sale, the fewer sales I make; and the less I need to make a sale, the more sales I make. Still, you can't let your needs to sell override your need to do what's right for your customer.

This advice is especially important to remember when you approach the closing step.

I remember flying to San Francisco to make a call on a vice president of sales of an international company. The evening before, I walked by the company's headquarters and examined its thirty or so stories. Something unusual happened to me as I stood there. Deep inside me, a silent voice said, "I don't need to make this sale. I'm doing quite well as it is! I know I can help these people make a lot of money by building their sales organization. What I can do for them will be far greater than what they do for me."

I thought about this throughout the night. I began saying to myself,

"I don't *need* to make this sale! I *need* to help them, because they *need* the help that I can bring to them." I found that when I released myself from the need to make a sale, and focused on my responsibility to help this company—if they wanted help—all my negative feelings and fears of rejection and making a sale disappeared.

I approached and interviewed the decision maker, honestly attempting to find out if I could help them. I made the sale, the largest one I had ever made so far. Since then, I have enjoyed a very successful relationship with this organization.

Many times since then, I've said to myself, "I don't need to make this sale; I *need* to help this organization solve its problems." I quickly found that I began to make sales that were ten to twenty times the size of ones I'd been making. Very little had changed, except my own belief system and attitudes toward selling. My earnings increased proportionally—proving my belief that earnings come when we focus more on creating value for customers.

My sales multiplied when I replaced my need to make a sale with my need to help organizations increase sales and customer satisfaction.

I realize that you may be at a point where you actually *do* need to make a sale. I've been there; I've experienced the fear that "If I don't sell something today, they may turn my telephone off tonight."

It's not a pleasant feeling. But you can work through this fear by focusing on creating value for people. I've seen thousands of salespeople come and go, and I'm fully convinced that going through this difficult phase is the entry price to higher success in selling. Every salesperson experiences disappointments and difficult times. Success is usually determined by a commitment to working through these tough times.

Importance of Values and Feelings of Self-Worth

Your values and feelings of self-worth powerfully influence your closing abilities. When you adopt an *extra mile* philosophy that's genuinely held as an internal value, it soon expresses itself as an outer demonstrated behavior. When you are driven to give extra value because of who you are, rather than what you do to sell more, you'll achieve higher levels of prosperity and self-esteem, and better, long-lasting customer relationships.

Your feelings of self-worth reign supreme in influencing your emotions and subsequent behaviors. To an integrity salesperson, self-worth is measured by the amount of value you believe you create for others along with the expectation of high rewards. Your sales over time will be consistent with your inner feelings of worth. Your answer to the question "What level of success do I deserve?" influences your sales more than most any other factor.

I know that there are times when a bad economy and poor market conditions significantly influence sales. But usually these variables are temporary. And even in difficult times, great salespeople find a way to sell.

If you want to significantly increase your sales and personal success, you must continually strengthen your feelings of self-worth. And few things influence our external level of success more than the inner, unconscious pictures we hold of ourselves.

Until we change the pictures on the inside, nothing on the outside will change. Practicing the Action Guides of this book will help you do this—not by just *knowing*, but by *practicing*.

How to Change Your Self-Pictures

Most of this book is designed to help you develop an appropriate view of selling and a clear view of your own abilities—bringing these into congruence with your values, activities, and belief in your product or service.

Here are some actions that can help change your internal images of *who* you are and *what* level of success you think is possible for you to enjoy:

1.   Spend twenty minutes each day clearly visualizing in great detail the person you'd like to become.

2. Take the first ten minutes and write on an index card, *How can I create more value for more people than I've been doing?* Write this out, then close your eyes and think. As you ask this question and listen to yourself, write down every idea that comes into your mind. If nothing comes, don't worry—just keep doing the exercise for ten minutes first thing each morning.

3. Eventually ideas will begin to come to you through hunches, spur-of-the-moment ideas, or awake-in-the-middle-of-the-night thoughts. Write these down without evaluation.

4. Spend the second ten minutes thinking of specific actions you can take today.

After thirty days of consciously practicing these four suggestions, you'll begin to feel and see results. You'll begin to focus on creating more value for more people. As this happens, you'll become more and more valuable to your customers. This will result in your feeling more confident, or valuable, to yourself. You'll expand your self-respect, which will enable you to enjoy greater customer respect.

Soon, your entire view of who you are and what level of prosperity and success you deserve to reach will naturally and smoothly expand, and your sales and customer relationships will increase.

Keep a Close Check on Your Ego

Let's face it, most of us who sell have substantial egos.

Selling is a tonic for our egos. Closing sales gives us a high. This is one basic fact that I've noticed about successful salespeople. In many cases, this "selling high" surpasses money, recognition, or rewards as main motivation.

Ego can be a creative force within us or a destructive one. It's influenced by our level of self-esteem, emotional intelligence, and values.

It's the rare salesperson who hasn't allowed his ego to prevent him from closing. Egos can jump up at several points of a sale, but especially at the negotiating and closing steps.

I speak from experience when I say that egos can ruin sales.

I remember getting a call one day from a regional vice president of a major life insurance company. He had implemented our Integrity Selling program, and after six months had enjoyed more than a 20 percent sales increase. He was so excited that he wanted me to go to New York and talk to the director of training and development, and volunteered to call and set up an appointment.

I went to New York for a 2:00 P.M. appointment, and arrived at the reception area about ten minutes early. Soon I was taken into the director's office and told that he would be in soon.

Soon, 2:30 came, then 3:00. At about 3:30, the man came in. Seeing me sitting in his office, he said in a rather authoritative voice, "What in the hell are you doing in my office?"

I thought he was saying this in jest, so I responded with "Oh, I'm just hanging out."

I quickly found out that he wasn't joking.

"Why are you here?" he asked, in an almost hostile tone.

I told him about my appointment and that their regional person had used our course and wanted me to talk to him about it.

"We already have one," he quickly responded. Then he spent the next twenty minutes almost screaming at me, using frequent profanities, insisting that I was imposing on his time.

It became obvious that I wasn't developing any kind of warm, fuzzy rapport with him.

After several minutes he asked, "Why do you think we'd even be interested in your program?"

"Because your Southeastern Region had around a 20 percent increase in sales after implementing it."

"We have our own training program," he replied.

"Yes sir, I know, the people in the Southeast told me about it, and said it wasn't very good."

His nose, ears, and face got as red as a neon sign.

"I designed our present sales training course," he shot back.

Knowing that I didn't have a chance of going any further, and after allowing him to scream and berate me, I replied in a very soft voice, "Then that would explain why it doesn't work!"

After saying this, I picked up my materials and walked out, leaving him in a state of stunned catatonia.

Did I win? No! Did he win? No. I could have helped his company. No one won.

Although I really had no chance of making a sale, I could tell you about many other calls where I didn't make a sale because my ego jumped in.

I learned this lesson: Egos controlled can be creative motivators. Egos uncontrolled can block us from being true customer advocates.

A healthy ego says to customers, "It isn't about me, it's about creating value for you." An unhealthy one says, "It's about my selling you something."

How to Know When You've Completed the Close Step

1.   Everyone's concerns have been successfully worked through.
2.   They understand how the benefits of your product or service will exceed their cost.
3.   They want what you have.
4.   They're ready to take the appropriate closing action.

How to Gain the Most from This Chapter

Read this chapter three times this week. As you do, ask and answer these questions:

1. What has been my view of closing?
2. When it comes time to ask for a decision, what emotions do I feel?
3. Does what I've been taught about closing conflict with any of my values, self-beliefs, or sense of right or wrong?
4. When I'm doing the right thing for customers, do my confidence and expectations grow stronger?
5. Can I distance myself from the need to make a sale and focus on the value I can give customers?
6. Do I believe in the profit motive? Do I feel that it's right for me to be highly compensated when I create high value for customers?

Look over the following self-suggestions and write them on index cards. Carry and repeat them to yourself daily. Say them to yourself fifty times in the morning and fifty times in the afternoon.

- *When I do the right thing for people, saying "yes" is the right thing for them to do!*
- *Every day, in every way, I'm creating more value for more people.*
- *I am surrounded by incredible opportunities to help my customers.*
- *I only have to increase my service to others to increase my prosperity.*
- *I build my own self-respect by serving and respecting others.*
- *The more value I create for people, the more personal rewards I'll enjoy.*

You can program new self-beliefs in your "I Am" by the repeated suggestion of these statements, or by designing others that address your individual needs. Continually repeating these statements will help you grow and become a stronger, more successful person.

Your ability to close larger sales is mainly an issue of the programming in your "I Am" that defines *who* you believe you are, and *what* you believe you're capable of achieving, rather than any strategies or techniques.

Remember, it's with your "I Think" that you initiate action. Choose to take the actions that I have recommended each day, and within a few weeks you'll gradually reprogram your "I Am" with new automatic habits. This will then trigger new emotions of confidence, courage, energy, and expectations of higher performance in your "I Feel."

In a very short time, you'll no longer settle for old goals. You'll enjoy an enlarged view of your future possibilities. Your life will never be the same again.

But I must warn you. Don't expect these wonderful blessings to happen to you simply because you've read this book. They won't. They will, however, happen to you as you faithfully practice the concepts, Action Guides, and principles I've shared with you.

Success will come to you as you practice, practice, practice.

Afterword

Emerson once wrote, *No man can learn what he has not preparation for learning.*

The truth is that we *hear* what we're prepared to *hear*. We *learn* what we're prepared to *learn*. We *discover* and *comprehend* what we're prepared to *discover* and *comprehend*.

I hope that reading this book has prepared you to learn much more about your actual capabilities and possibilities. That it has brought you face-to-face with the highly effective person that you are, and that it has kindled an ongoing desire within you to continue growing, so that higher success is an ever-evolving journey in your life.

I challenge you to go back now and spend a week on each chapter. Focus on practicing the ideas and Action Guides. As you practice these ideas, you'll align yourself with powerful, energizing, psychic forces of *integrity*. The physical and emotional congruence that you develop will then transform and multiply your personal and relationship powers. Your *area of the possible* will continually expand.

Nothing will ensure your personal, professional, and corporate success more than striving for greater truth, genuine sincerity, and your dedication to creating more value for people.

Take a moment and reflect on the wise words of Anthony Hope:

> In the deep, unwritten wisdom of life, there are many things to be
> learned that cannot be taught. We never know them by hearing them

spoken, but grow into them by experience, and recognize them through understanding. Understanding is a great experience in itself, but it does not come through instruction.

You'll only learn *what's* in this book when you take *action* and *experience* it. Just reading about it isn't enough.

So keep reading and practicing. Recognize, relate, assimilate, and apply these success principles. Don't be content with just learning. Demand of yourself that you make these concepts a part of your automatic sales habits.

Your success, your sales, your self-esteem, and your overall prosperity will skyrocket as you make Integrity Selling your moral and ethical guideline for the way you sell.

Index